PRINCE IZON

A ROMANCE OF
THE GRAND CANYON

PRINCE IZON

A ROMANCE OF THE GRAND CANYON

JAMES PAUL KELLY

WILDSIDE PRESS

PRINCE IZON

Published by Wildside Press LLC.
www.wildsidebooks.com

A HINT

To those who read as they run, this work may lack the conventional moral of the wicked being punished in all cases and of the just being rewarded in proportion.

The Esoteric, those who read between the lines, may perhaps find a hidden meaning that reveals a significance of profound interest to themselves.

—THE AUTHOR

PROLOGUE

IN the heart of the continent of North America, there lies a region of mystery, a strange and wonderful locality, utterly unlike any other part of the globe, and so little explored that it is almost unknown to our ninety millions of people, except the few courageous ones who have attempted to penetrate its forbidding and hidden ways.

For it is a region of terrific dangers, yet of majestic grandeurs. To stand on its brink is to behold a scene vouchsafed nowhere else on this earth — a panorama so stupendous in its extent and bewildering in its depth, that, at the first view, the breath is bound and the brain reels; a vision perhaps more vast and alluring than the one spread before the Son of Man, when tempted by Lucifer on the heights.

To descend to its abysmal depths and attempt to navigate the torrent that fights its way through its Plutonian channels, is to encounter a real inferno more awesome than the one imagined by Dante and pictured by Doré.

From these depths, to gaze to the empyrean, is to

PROLOGUE

behold a blend of vividly stratified colors, gorgeously illumined clouds, and delicately tinted skies; a blend of such unearthly and ineffable radiance that the beholder is enchanted with a hint of what might be the portals of paradise. It is a chaos of abysses profound and heights tremendous, of titanic labyrinths and untrodden and forbidding fastnesses.

Such is the Grand Canyon of Arizona.

CONTENTS

CHAPTER		PAGE
I	THE MIRAGE	13
II	THE GRAND CANYON	22
III	THE MYSTERY OF THE AZTECS	30
IV	A STRANGE INVITATION	39
V	PASSING THE BARRIER	45
VI	IN THE DRAG NET	52
VII	PRINCE IZON THE MIGHTY	63
VIII	PLEASANT DAYS	74
IX	TOPELTZIN OUTLINES HIS PLOT	82
X	THE VOICE FROM THE PLATEAU	92
XI	LUXTOL, THE PEARL CITY	101
XII	LOVE'S TELEGRAPH	112
XIII	ON THE PARAPET	121
XIV	IN THE LABYRINTH	134
XV	THE HAIL DANCE	142
XVI	BY MOONLIGHT	164
XVII	ZENO'S LITTLE GAME	173
XVIII	DELIVERANCE AT HAND	183
XIX	THE FIGHT IN THE GROTTO	195
XX	THE REVOLT OF ZILPAN	202
XXI	THE NIGHT BEFORE THE FESTIVAL	212

CONTENTS—*Continued*

Chapter		Page
XXII	THE MASKED FESTIVAL	219
XXIII	FRIENDS IN THE DARK	228
XXIV	TLAX AND ZULM	240
XXV	TEZCATLIPOCA LISTENS	250
XXVI	PRINCE IZON — TRAITOR	257
XXVII	UNMASKED	267
XXVIII	THE BETRAYAL	277
XXIX	TEMPTATION	286
XXX	THE THIRD CANDIDATE	298
XXXI	THE LAST TEMPTATION	314
XXXII	THE RED ROOM	326
XXXIII	AT SUNRISE	333
XXXIV	THE BLESSING OF THE TROOPS	338
XXXV	A SOLEMN REPROOF	345
XXXVI	ON THE TEOCOLLI — PAGANISM	350
XXXVII	ON THE TEOCOLLI — HEROISM	357
XXXVIII	ON THE TEOCOLLI — DESPERATION	364
XXXIX	THE BATTLE AT THE GATES	371
XL	ON THE TEOCOLLI—OMNIPOTENCE	385
XLI	THE LAST VICTIM	396

ILLUSTRATIONS

	PAGE
BLACK EAGLE ON GUARD	50
ON THE PARAPET — TOPELTZIN'S MAGIC	130
MARIAM BEFORE IZON	306
THE FIGHT ON THE TEOCOLLI	360

PRINCE IZON
A ROMANCE OF THE GRAND CANYON

CHAPTER I
THE MIRAGE

"A MIRAGE!" cried Professor Raymon.
His daughter and her cousin, who were unpacking a hamper, looked up at the exclamation and stood spellbound. Mariam gazed with parted lips upon this marvellous spectacle of the skies. Isabel clenched her hands upon her bosom, while she flushed, then paled. The Indian servants, making camp, were awed, too, standing like bronze images. It was new even to them, this wonder of wonders, though they had always lived in this wild environment, which was the Buckskin Plateau, within a mile of the rim of the Grand Canyon.

It was not surprising that the members of the party were dumb with amazement. It was no mere freak

PRINCE IZON

of fantastic cloud formation that confronted them, but the reflection of an actual city, built apparently against a high cliff, its buildings rising tier upon tier, following in picturesque lines the windings of the cliff.

Every detail stood out with the clearness of an immense stereoscopic view. A strange thing about it, however, and the one thing which held the professor's gaze and exalted him beyond his self-possession, was the fact that this city was like no known place on earth; its architecture was of a character not to be found in any spot upon the globe, unless in ruins. Its wide streets, its rows of edifices, its gardens, shelved back, terrace upon terrace, and its bridges all were portrayed with vivid fidelity. Professor Raymon, to whom the architecture was as familiar as his own birthplace, could not repress his emotion.

As the vision disappeared, there stood against the sky a cross of gigantic size. It was the last of the cloud city to show, and it had a yellow sheen as of gold. In a moment it was gone, and when the breathless girls turned, they found Professor Raymon with bared and bowed head.

"It is more than an image," he said devoutly. "It

THE MIRAGE

is a revelation, a blessing upon my life's work, and a promise of its fulfilment."

Mariam looked at him with a start.

"Father!" she exclaimed, "you don't mean—why, you must mean that this is a mirage of the Aztec city that for years it has been your ambition to find?"

"I do," he replied. "The architecture is the same that I noted at the ruins of Mitla; the same that still crumbles upon the plateaus conquered by Cortez; the same that once stood in old Mexico, under the Montezumas. In a word, we have just seen the reflection of an Aztec city, and all my theories are proved!"

Exclamations among the carriers caused them to turn, and sweeping toward them they saw a band of mounted men. As the swift cavalcade approached, the girls were terrified to see a company of Indians, in native costumes of barbaric brightness. They were riding abreast in a long line and in advance was a tall rider on a black horse. Seeing the girls frightened, Professor Raymon, with a reassuring smile, laid a hand upon the shoulder of each.

The broad line swept toward them until it seemed that they would surely be run down, the girls with great difficulty restraining their impulse to fly, when, at a command from the leader, the wild band came to a sudden halt, the horses drawn back on their haunches. The leader swung gracefully to the ground, and the girls were astonished to see the professor dash forward, meeting this tall, finely modelled savage half way. There was an exchange of guttural words between the two men. They shook hands, and the professor bared his left forearm. The Indian clasped his hand upon the scar thus shown, and at the same time the professor clasped a similar scar upon the Indian's forearm. The simple ceremony, a token of the blood-brothership that had been sealed between them years before when a trace of the life current of each was transferred into the veins of the other, was a profound mystery to the girls.

"I knew when I wrote you that you would come," said the professor, speaking in English. "I want you, if you can, to accompany me on an exploring trip."

"Now?" asked the chief.

"If you can; I have brought along such necessities as we shall require."

For answer the Indian turned to his silent and motionless braves. He gave a command in their tongue.

THE MIRAGE

A stalwart young fellow rode forward. An explanation, another command, and the brightly decked warriors wheeled, the entire line bounding forward and sweeping away as rapidly as it had come. It was a swift, graceful manœuvre, full of the free, savage life of the plains.

"And now, brother," said the Indian in English, "I am yours to do as you see fit."

"Good!" exclaimed the professor. "First I wish to introduce you to my daughter and my niece. This, girls, is my blood-brother, Black Eagle, who saved my life many years ago."

He followed this with a formal introduction in Spanish, and the girls were surprised to find their visitor responding in the same tongue, with a speech of pleasant courtesy. The contrast was so striking that they were almost embarrassed. Black Eagle was clad in sandals, breeching, and cloak of fine material and workmanship, and a head-dress of handsome plumes, significant of his chieftainship. He was tall, erect, built upon lines of athletic grace and strength. His face, cast in the mould of his race, was keenly intelligent. He had received exceptional advantages in the way of training and culture, a splendid type of the modern educated Indian. Isabel, in whose veins there flowed the blood of an Indian princess who had married one of the Dons under Cortez, was the first to recover her ease, quickly forgetting her confusion in her admiration, while Mariam was aglow with appreciation of this remarkable friend of her father's.

When they were seated at luncheon, the professor explained to Black Eagle the purpose of his trip; but Black Eagle shook his head.

"I don't like to discourage you," he said, "but I fear you will have only your labor for your pains. The Havasupai Indians have lived in these parts for generations; as their chief, I have travelled and explored much, and I may say that, aside from the apparently inaccessible portions of the great chasm, there is no place which could contain such a city as you mention."

Professor Raymon smiled indulgently. "I hope, by pitting my long course of reasoning against your material knowledge, to convince you."

"I trust you will," replied Black Eagle courteously. "A mirage is more than curious. There is a tradition in my tribe that many great side canyons have been seen in mirages, but they never could be found. Mirages have reproduced scenes that were hidden beyond the curvature of the earth, consequently this cloud city may have been at any distance."

Professor Raymon laid his hand affectionately upon Black Eagle's shoulder. "I invite you to share with me the pleasure of the discovery that I feel I am about to make. That is why I sent you word from Flagstaff, and by this you see what I think of my blood-brother."

Black Eagle flushed with pleasure, and the girls looked from him to the professor with undisguised interest.

"The blood-brother, father?" inquired Mariam. "You told me when I was a child about this ceremony, but I never expected to meet the young man who had saved your life."

"It is one of the most pleasurable incidents in my memory," replied the professor, "although at the time it was a serious one. I had come from Mexico to the United States to take the chair of archæology in a Western college and met Black Eagle, then merely a boy, at a Pima Indian cattle round-up. I was riding in front of a herd when I was flung from my horse

PRINCE IZON

through his stumbling into a gopher hole. Seeing me afoot, the steers charged me. At the risk of his life, Black Eagle galloped across the front of the herd, and reaching down, snatched me from the ground. I learned then that a man on horseback may go freely among cattle that would rend him to pieces if he were on foot; I learned too of the bravery of which a man of unbroken ancestry is capable. If the Havasupai Indians are descended from the lost tribes of Israel, as is maintained by many scientists, then Black Eagle is a descendant from those tribes."

An exclamation from Isabel caused them to turn again to that quarter of the sky in which they had beheld the mirage. Now, over all that space, from the horizon to the zenith, there glowed and wavered a rose-like radiance, which turned to orange, to green, to red, shifting and changing its pure transparent coloring, as if by some vast, supernal magic!

It was the reflection of the colored strata of the canyon upon the clouds of the upper air. Instead of the ordinary spectacle of fleecy white cumuli drifting overhead across a background of blue, these clouds were transformed into billows of brilliant coloring, a red

THE MIRAGE

cloud mingling with one of green, both followed by orange or copper, all of them slowly varying their tints as they swept over the reflected colors from the canyon strata. This spectacle is too vast, too gorgeous, too far beyond the limits of human vision to be seen elsewhere upon this earth.

CHAPTER II
THE GRAND CANYON

THE following morning, the party approached the canyon with keen curiosity, not unmixed with disappointment on the part of the girls, for, up to its very brink, there was nothing to indicate its existence, only the usual features of every forest glade being encountered.

The Indian servants had been sent away. Not caring to have witnesses to his discoveries, if any should be made, Professor Raymon had taken a journey south of the direction usually followed by tourists. He had then cached quantities of stores, and now three burros bore all of the supplies deemed needful.

Mariam and her father were in advance as they approached the brink, Isabel walking with Black Eagle and admiring more his deep voice than the weird legend of the canyon he was narrating. It was a gruesome tale, well fitted to prepare her for what she was soon to see; how in past days a fierce tribe had inhabited

THE GRAND CANYON

this plateau; how they executed their prisoners by lashing them to a pole and, with a warrior at each end, swinging the victim back and forth out over the precipice where it descended a sheer half-mile; how stoic braves, thus tortured, warriors who would glory in uttering no sound at the fiery stake, would melt and become as whimpering babes before the final swing.

Black Eagle's narrative was interrupted by a scream from Mariam. She had reached the brink, had instantly thrown her hands up to cover her eyes, and had swayed dizzily against her father, leaning against his encircling arm.

Startled and full of solicitude, Isabel ran forward, and it was thus that suddenly and without warning the unearthly spectacle burst upon her.

She was overwhelmed with awe; she stood spellbound by the wonderful sight. The earth upon which they stood abruptly ended. They could go no farther without stepping into space. Cleft away at their feet was the world in which they were born, and with which they were familiar, and extending before their amazed vision was a new world, strangely fearful and yet strangely beautiful.

P R I N C E   I Z O N

It was a region of chaotic and bewildering immensity; of colossal pyramids; of titanic temples; of tremendous precipices; of mighty Cyclopean formations tinted with the hues of the rainbow, swathed in billows of rolling clouds and reflecting colors more gorgeous than those of the most brilliant aurora.

None but those who have viewed this stupendous scene can comprehend the awe with which the girls were enthralled by the panorama spread before them. With bated breath they stood, conscious of nothing but the wondrous sight and absorbing as far as they could this marvellous work of the Creator, the most wonderful scene in the world.

No language could describe the immensity and grandeur of this area of primordial chaos. The glories of the views as they unfolded were so beautiful and withal so sublime, that Mariam first gave voice to the hosannas swelling in their hearts, murmuring,

"*Oh, wondrous Nature! Scene sublime!*
Glorious work of the Divine!"

"See yonder golden cloud rolling away from that temple-like structure!" cried Isabel. "Why, it is grander than Karnak could have been."

THE GRAND CANYON

"Karnak!" repeated the professor. "That great Egyptian structure was but a pigmy to this. The pyramids would seem puny if placed within it; but all measurements here are titanic. That plateau upon the opposite rim of the canyon is over twelve miles away. The water you see looking like a rivulet, is a torrent two hundred yards wide. Those cliffs yonder, forming the banks of the inner canyon, are two thousand feet high, and the river itself is more than a mile below the level where we are standing. When you look up and down the canyon your view reaches over forty miles."

"Look!" exclaimed Isabel again. "Have you noticed that cloud which was golden when it rolled away from our 'temple'? It is now a gorgeous crimson!"

"And that is by no means the last of its transformations," replied the professor. "That is one of the greatest fascinations of the scene; never is the coloring the same; infinite variety, yet always infinite beauty and sublimity; who could accomplish this wonder but the Omnipotent?"

Silently they gazed for a time, absorbed in their emotions, until at last the professor aroused them.

PRINCE IZON

"Come," he said simply, and led the way down the trail that Black Eagle had found for him.

Mariam and Isabel lingered only long enough to take one last look at the magnificent scene they were leaving, and as their eyes absorbed all the glorious view they little realized that they were never to look down upon it again.

Professor Raymon, who under this modest name in the United States hid his Mexican title and rank of Don Ramon Navarez, had wisely chosen the place which was to prove the startling theory that, after all, seemed so logical when explained to Black Eagle later in the day. As for the girls, he had so imbued them with the romantic possibilities that they had eagerly demanded the privilege of accompanying him.

A few brave men, heroes every one, have succeeded in traversing the Grand Canyon from source to mouth. Many more have perished. Their explorations have been of necessity only superficial, as the terrific dangers attending this trip are such that merely to go through the main canyon, without exploring the side fissures, is in itself a remarkable feat. Many portions, accessible from the upper plateaus, have been traversed.

THE GRAND CANYON

Professor Raymon, having brought all these data together, and casting out one locality after another, had at last settled upon this chasm as the only logical one fulfilling all the conditions of his problem. It was an unexplored side canyon of an immensity only to be guessed at, which branched out from an extremely hazardous portion of the river. Nothing was known of this beyond its enormous extent, save that from the sound it was judged that a waterfall, probably larger than the Bridal Veil Falls, there poured down its cataract. So far as anything further was known of this branch of the main canyon, it might have been upon another planet.

A trail, never trodden before by white men who had returned to tell of it, led by winding ways down the precipices, over mesas into abysses; led, also, right into the midst of those signs and tokens that the professor had been seeking; and as the party progressed proof piled upon proof. The extensive ruins of a city spread over a mesa, told the tale of an experiment, abandoned perhaps because its location was too accessible to the predatory tribes on the plains above. Picture writings upon high cliffs attested a skill which has been a mystery for centuries, for these symbols, painted upon walls, overhung by ledges, are inaccessible by ropes from above, and by reason of their sheer, smooth drop of hundreds of feet, seem equally inaccessible from below by any wingless creature; and the Aztecs only have left these monuments to their intelligence and enterprise.

Throughout the day's journey there were new wonders and new revelations until at last, just before nightfall, the little party reached the banks of the river that welcomed them with its ceaseless rumble.

The men were expert campers, and the girls were soon comfortably installed in their tent. They quickly prepared an appetizing supper, which was enjoyed in the cheerful glow of the camp fire. All were in the most exuberant spirits. Professor Raymon and Black Eagle began a laughing dispute, in which the girls joined with flippant suggestions, as to the best way to tether the burros and the most scientific method of pegging and bracing the tents.

But the light chatter came to seem out of place amid the majesty of their surroundings. At their feet rushed the dark, swiftly moving river. On either side towering cliffs reached apparently to the dusking skies. Up and

THE GRAND CANYON

down the canyon were shadows that blended and deepened into impenetrable blackness, where misty forms seemed to rise and hover, gigantic genii of this Plutonian highway, and over all, save for that insistent murmur of the mighty stream, brooded the profound silence of the underworld.

CHAPTER III

THE MYSTERY OF THE AZTECS

"IT was upon such a beautiful June night as this that you and I first met, Black Eagle," musingly began the professor after a long, thoughtful silence, "and I was then, as now, upon the track of this Aztec race. I had journeyed this way for the purpose of seeing the Pima Indian pottery, finding it identical with the Aztec. Inquiries revealed a tradition that, generations back, a great race from the south had passed through their land and left this trace; that they had come from the lower river and the great gulf; that they bore numerous treasures with them, and were of a refined character far different from and superior to the tribes hereabout. While I was with the Pimas the Havasupais came to visit them; and gave me a life-long friend in yourself."

"I cannot yet see," said Black Eagle, "how you deduced your theory. It seems to me that Prescott very effectually disposed of the Aztecs."

"But how?" retorted the professor. "When Pres-

MYSTERY OF THE AZTECS

cott was done with his history of the conquest of Mexico he had merely evaded the great mystery of the age. The Aztecs have the most romantic history of any nation in the world. They were a proud, progressive, warlike race, well versed in the arts and sciences. Their gold work has never been surpassed, nor their feather work equalled. They had a government well nigh perfect in all its workings, marriage institutions of flawless purity, a home life of gentle happiness. They had unified the tribes they had encountered in their upward sweep from the south, and when Cortez with his powerful army of allies attacked them, he destroyed a civilization that, but for one exception, might have leavened this whole continent. The banner that Cortez carried, however, was irresistible. The Cross had come to conquer and the sign of the flaming sun was doomed to give way before it. Their fight with the Spaniards is of little interest now; the fact which caught my attention was this extremely significant one. Prescott says, seventy thousand of them in a body evacuated the city of Mexico with the honors of war, 'going west.' There were at least half as many who had left during the siege, carrying their treasures with them, so that it is safe to assume that at least one hundred thousand of them were banded together. There lies the mystery. What became of them? Pestilence could not have wiped them out without leaving its scar upon history; they were not exterminated, or legend would tell us that; they did not intermarry; they built no cities. Mitla was their former capital. Examine a map of old Mexico, almost the whole of which was once under the dominion of the Montezumas, and you will immediately pick out, as the only possible westward course, the lower sweep of the Gulf of California. In a word, the Aztecs were driven to the sea. Not being a seagoing nation it would never occur to them to attempt the building of large ships to brave the terrors of the ocean. They were, however, expert in the building and use of small caiques or canoes, as Cortez found out to his cost on the high lakes surrounding the old city of Mexico. Their natural course, therefore, would be to build small boats with which to cruise along the coast until they should find an inviting landing.

"By this time they were doubtless tired of conflict. They had already fought themselves into preëminence, as the dominating nation, before Cortez came upon them, and they had even then begun to lay war aside, for the quieter conquests of science and art. Now, all they desired was a peaceful country where they might build anew the glories that they had lost.

"In this pilgrimage I have little doubt that they carried the son of Montezuma, who is so summarily dismissed and left in mystery by a single sentence in Prescott's history, to the effect that at the beginning of the invasion, Montezuma placed his son in hiding with the chief of the friendly Michogehans in the west. We know positively, now, that the fugitives did reach the coast; and that they did not cross the ocean is borne out by the fact that no other continent or group of islands in the world bears legends of this strange race landing among them. The possibility that they were lost at sea, if they attempted to cross it, is the only tenable one, and it is scarcely likely, even then, that all would be lost; moreover, to clinch the whole argument, there have been found, petrified in the sands of the upper reach of the Gulf of California, the keels and prows of several small boats, portions covered with hieroglyphs that are Aztec, proving that at least some members of the race must have reached that point. The rest is a simple conclusion. They coasted north along the inner tine of the gulf until they came to the mouth of the Colorado River. They ascended the canyon, and here have recently been found many of their hieroglyphs. We saw some to-day. Now, then, all these things being known, why not go a step further to the inevitable deduction? Still hunting for a locality inaccessible to the outside world, why may we not conclude that in this vast unknown region they have built and thriven? I am satisfied that we are near, if not their present abiding place, at least where they cast their last anchor to die. If they have perished, we shall soon learn it; but if they live, let us discover them. Black Eagle's own people, the Havasupai, have inhabited for centuries one of these canyons without assistance from the outside world; then why not these vigorous Aztecs? There are portions of this vast canyon untrodden by man, inaccessible, impenetrable, forbidden! Who shall say that I, or you, my children, will not be permitted to lift this veil between the ancient and the modern civilization?"

"All I can say," replied Black Eagle, "is that if your reasoning proves correct, you will have accomplished a feat as great as the astronomer who in his study, without the aid of telescope or other instruments, proved by mathematics the existence of a huge planet unseen by man and predicted the day and hour when it could be observed, through telescopes directed to a certain point in the sky. At the time named, the planet now called Neptune was viewed for the first time by man, and the astronomical world was not more astounded than the outer world will be if your theories are verified. I thank you in the name of my people for letting one of their race share in such an honor."

A hearty grasp of the hand by the professor was his only answer and then at his quiet order, "Now to rest," the party disposed themselves for the night.

Lulled to slumber by the murmur of the waters, and in the radiance of the moon which wrought its ever-changing, fantastic splendors in that abyss of mystery, the travellers slept soundly until the dawn of the day that was to be a vital one in their lives.

Once more their eyes awoke upon new marvels of light and shade and color, as the rising sun spread his flaming glories upon the sky and the tinted strata. Each new turn of the trail revealed new vistas, while with added ruggedness the path became more difficult.

At last they were compelled to pause, blocked. The trail upon the other side of the river stretched up the canyon, however. Professor Raymon took a package from the back of one of the burros. It proved to be a collapsible boat. In this they crossed the stream, the girls nervously apprehensive of the cataract that roared below them and of the shifting eddies on every hand, whirlpools which, formed in the swift constricted stream by sunken boulders, are the dangerous obstacles that have drawn down nearly all the craft bold enough to brave their dangers, and to make the navigation of the Colorado almost impossible.

The burros were tethered and left upon the other side for the time being, while the party examined new picture writings which they found around a bend of the trail. Suddenly the sky became overcast, and a violent rain storm followed. Some jutting cliffs afforded temporary shelter, but, owing to the immense shedding of the water into the river, the stream arose many feet in as many minutes, engulfing the burros. Before the men could reach it, the boat too was torn away by a drifting tree and carried down the raging stream.

The men, realizing that all was lost without the

boat, rushed down the bank hoping to recover it. In dismay Mariam and Isabel watched them. They saw Professor Raymon plunge into the torrent and finally reach the boat, into which he clambered; but the oars had been swept away and he was compelled to drift helplessly down that fatal stream where so many noble lives had already been lost. To their horror they saw the boat drawn towards the cataract. Though Professor Raymon appeared to be earnestly waving Black Eagle back, the chieftain plunged in to his rescue and both were swept out of sight. For a moment the girls stood panic-stricken; then, screaming, they ran down the trail to the edge of the cataract itself. There was no trace of men or boat, the latter having been drawn down by one of the maelstroms of the river.

The only answer to their cries of dismay was the mocking roar of the ceaselessly rushing water.

The miseries which came upon Mariam and Isabel the succeeding hours, are indescribable. Crouching under the precipice which was their only refuge from the rain, they slept little during the night, and spent their waking hours in tearful prayer. Dawn found them utterly desolate, and they wandered down the

PRINCE IZON

banks of the river, clinging to a desperate hope that their protectors might have escaped and that they would find them. They had almost abandoned themselves to despair, when the sound of voices down the stream caused them to thrill with expectation.

CHAPTER IV

A STRANGE INVITATION

A PARTY of men came into view around the bend of the trail. They were about thirty in number and attired like miners or prospectors; but with the first view of them the grief-stricken cousins gave up hope. Neither of their protectors was with the party. The costumes of the strangers, while made for rough service, differed in many respects from any the girls had ever seen. Their leader stopped as he reached the ledge, under which the girls had crouched in order to observe without being observed. Unaware of their presence he turned to his companions and addressed them in a language unknown to Mariam and Isabel and with gestures that seemed to indicate that they contemplated crossing the river. A boulder, accidentally loosened by the girls, rolled down the cliff; knowing they would be discovered, they stepped out from under the ledge. Mariam, feeling that in simple courage lay their best hope, with an inward prayer that he might understand the language, addressed him in Spanish.

"Señor," she said, "my father and his companion were lost in the river yesterday, and oh, Señor — " sobs choked her utterance.

The man, who had already removed his hat, now bowed to her with courtliness and deep compassion.

"And you wish of course to ask us if we have seen or heard of them," he finished for her in excellent Spanish. "I deeply regret that we have not, but if we can be of aid to you in any way, my companions and myself are at your service, to any extent. Where and how did it happen?"

Isabel, whom he now addressed, though herself almost beyond control with grief, gave him the details of their misfortune, and, while she did so, would have had an excellent opportunity to form an opinion of their new acquaintance had she been less deeply sorrowful. Although roughly attired, his superb physique could not be hidden, and as he stood with uncovered head he gave a curious impression that this garb was one to which he was unused. Had he been clad in the conventional dress of civilization, he would have been one of the most strikingly handsome of manly men. Nobility and refinement sat upon him like a royal vestment,

A STRANGE INVITATION

and the gentleness and kindly modulation of his voice, as he made interested inquiries, stamped him as one who had not only birth and breeding but innate qualities of his own to make him worth the faith of any man or the trust of any woman. His action was prompt and decisive. He was already dividing his following into search parties, when their attention was attracted by a shout down the stream. It was from a straggling detachment of the same band, and as they came up it was seen that they were carrying an unconscious form, which proved to be that of Black Eagle. They had found him on the bank, where he had become exhausted after escaping the cataract; hidden beyond a small ridge of boulders, he had escaped the eyes of those in advance.

His presence revived the hopes of the girls, and, though they had known him so short a time, he was already so intimately bound up with their present interests that they found their hearts going out to him as to one who had been loved and lost. Isabel, who carried at her belt a small handbag, knelt by him and from a flask moistened his lips and bathed his temples. Under this treatment he soon revived, and an eager light flashed into his eyes as they opened upon Isabel bending over him. He clasped her hand and endeavored to rise. When he had been helped to do so he turned to Mariam, who had not yet spoken, but who stood, pale as death, her hands clenched at her sides, with parted lips awaiting his first words. As he saw her attitude his throat seemed to swell with pain, and tears moistened his lashes.

"It was no use," he said brokenly, in answer to her mute appeal. "I bring you no good news. I could not save him."

For the first time Mariam's fortitude deserted her, and uttering a despairing cry, she fainted in the arms of Isabel. The one with whom they had talked sprang to Isabel's assistance, and tenderly helped to lay Mariam down upon the bank, on which cloaks had been hastily spread. Then, while Isabel worked over her, he stood apart with a companion.

"What beauty!" he exclaimed. "Never in my dreams have I beheld the like. My quest is ended."

When Mariam had revived and was able to compose herself, the leader approached.

"You will, perhaps, wish to return by the route you came, but I know that you will not care to leave the

A STRANGE INVITATION

locality of the canyon at present. I shall have watchers posted down the river for two or three days, and in the meantime I beg you to accept our hospitality in a city not far from here."

"Then there is a city!" Black Eagle exclaimed. "Why, it seems incredible, although our lost companion insisted that one was concealed somewhere in this canyon."

"Then I have a surprise in store for you," replied the leader. "There is not only one city, in a tributary canyon less than ten hours' journey from here, but there are two, known as the Pearl City and the Red City, and I can promise you a most hospitable welcome to the one in which I live."

Isabel felt doubtful about this proposal, and a glance from Black Eagle told her that he too had misgivings; but Mariam gave the matter no heed whatever. She was so stunned by her grief that she could have been led like a child by any one in whom she saw trustworthiness, and she had not even noticed the absorbed attention the strange young man was bestowing upon her. Had she done so, doubtless his dark eyes, sparkling with vivacity, would have seemed to conceal

PRINCE IZON

no duplicity in their clear depths, and his manner, earnestly chivalrous, would have impressed her with profound trust. As Black Eagle and Isabel stood pondering the matter there came from the upper canyon the sound of a distant swelling chorus, low yet distinct. Beautiful and wonderful was it to these lost and sorrowful wanderers, as it was borne softly to them from an almost incredible distance through this vast, natural sound channel!

"Sanctus! Sanctus! Sanctus! Dominus Deus Sabaoth!
Pleani sunt coeli et terra!
Gloria! Gloria! tua! Hosanna in Excelsis!"

CHAPTER V

PASSING THE BARRIER

AS the grand old anthem, so familiar to them and yet so strange in these surroundings, swelled upon the air, distinct, yet faint and sweet as if it might have been wafted from some distant, angelic chorus, it was like a new invitation that seemed to banish all doubt and uncertainty, and yet to reassure the bereft ones of the integrity of this pleasant stranger. Seeing their wonder, he waited listening until the anthem had ceased, until there ensued that silence which music-lovers know, the tense silence that vibrates still with echoes lower and sweeter than the mere human ear can grasp.

"To-day is the Lord's day," he explained, "and the song you hear is from the church choir in our beautiful Pearl City."

The companion at his side now raised a directing hand. It waved, and then a repetition of the hymn, low and reverent, arose from the men. They stood with heads bared and eyes turned to the sky, and the spirit

PRINCE IZON

of worship enfolded the little party like a benison, so that presently the sorrowful ones, forgetting that they were of a separate race and in a world entirely strange, remembering that they were all children of one great family, opened their souls to that higher comfort which alone can soothe the anguish of aching hearts. Their heartfelt praise of the power of the Creator, "Holy Lord God of Sabaoth! Thou filleth the heavens and the earth! Glory to Thee! Hosanna in the Highest!" was borne aloft through the quivering air of the canyon, to the very dome of heaven.

Again the music-haunted silence, and then once more the far-off, swelling chant.

There was need of no further argument or persuasion. With the tears trembling upon her lashes, Isabel turned to her host. He extended his hand.

"You will come, I know," he gently urged.

"We thank you," she answered simply. As they took up their march, their host introduced himself merely as one called Izon, and, though further introductions were necessarily brief, the girls were struck by the fact that all his immediate friends had a courtly refinement contrasting strangely with their rough attire.

PASSING THE BARRIER

The trail they now followed was a difficult one. The vast side canyon had held its isolation for so long because it was shut off from the main chasm by a natural barrier almost impenetrable, and even the plateaus above it were protected by yawning crevasses and ranges of rugged cliffs which were of no value to the roving bands of Indians that hunted and fought, and lived and died upon the surface. They crossed this barrier, following the secret trail which Izon knew. At nightfall, footsore and weary, they came upon a hut of logs and stone in which Mariam and Isabel were made as comfortable as possible, while the men pitched tents near by.

Travel had been so difficult during the day that there was little opportunity for conversation, but even without this the girls had noted that Izon was a person of much more importance than they had at first suspected, as his friends gave him unusual deference. About half the party were servants and carriers, and of the other half there were few who approached Izon on terms of anything like equality. Notwithstanding this, his bearing was one of uniform courtesy, even to the servants; and that he was a leader in addition to being a gentleman, was evinced by the fact that no detail of their march escaped him. No guide, no matter how far ahead, and no carrier, no matter how far behind, but came under his immediate supervision, from the time of their setting out until the servants had unpacked their bundles for the night camp and had prepared a supper that quite astonished the wanderers by its excellence. Black Eagle could not refrain from remarking upon this.

"Such elaborate preparations may seem a little unusual," confessed Izon, "but you will readily understand when I explain that the expedition was fitted out for quite an extensive hunt."

He said this with a whimsical earnestness that caused his nearest companion to smile, and though he had begun by addressing Black Eagle he quickly turned to Mariam. Finding her still absorbed in her sorrow, so that she neither listened nor ate, he spoke in the end directly to Isabel.

"Really," said she, "I feel badly about this. We are sorry to have interfered with your hunt."

Izon's friend who had smiled, now laughed outright, and it was not until some time later that the travellers learned the peculiar nature of this expedition, which had

PASSING THE BARRIER

come to an end the moment Izon realized Mariam's beauty. Izon cast a reproving glance upon his friend.

"Please give yourself no uneasiness on that score," he replied. "The river was too swollen to cross, and we would not have ventured it, after it had gone down, until my guides had studied the new eddies that form after every freshet."

Mariam sat just across the cloth from him, and attempting, wearily and mechanically, to give him the attention his speech demanded, she unconsciously gazed into his eyes, and he as unconsciously gazed into hers. Realization came to him suddenly, thrilling and strangely exulting him. Hastily shifting his glance, he caught that of his friend, upon whose countenance sat an expression so bantering and of such mischievous meaning that Izon found himself, without apparent cause, fairly blushing. His discomfiture was not abated to find that Mariam, without a trace of embarrassment, had calmly swept her gaze past him, not even aware that she had been staring at him. She was as one stricken by her bereavement, and if her eyes had noticed that this young man was good to look upon, her mind had taken no note of it.

PRINCE IZON

Izon, recovering himself, proved an entertaining talker, and Black Eagle thrilled with pride even as he sighed with sorrow that his blood-brother was not there to share this proof of every one of his theories. For Izon was a veritable Aztec, and he told them the legends and traditions of his people beginning far back beyond the invasion of Cortez; told of their struggle against savage tribes and inhospitable nature, and of their later triumphs. After supper he would have been content to talk on indefinitely in the hope that he might quicken the interest of one special listener, to the lightening of her woe if to no other end, had not his innate courtesy divined that the girls, less used to hardship than his followers, were well nigh exhausted. He therefore made it easy for them to escape to their much needed rest.

The closing of the door of the cabin increased their loneliness, and made more insistent their painful knowledge of the startling changes that had taken place in their lives. That they, nurtured as they had always been, used to luxury and shielded from every adverse wind, should be alone in the depths of this unknown world, surrounded by men of an alien race, seemed too

Black Eagle on Guard

PASSING THE BARRIER

great a calamity to be within the bounds of belief. It seemed like some strange dream from which they must soon awaken, to find themselves within the sheltered precincts of their own home. Alas, it was only too stern a reality! Somewhere on the surface of that rushing torrent, or caught beneath its waters, was the father whose great love and tenderness had always surrounded and guarded Mariam, the uncle who had taken Isabel as another daughter into the same protection, and it was not strange that this one great, overwhelming fact should blot out every thought, leaving the cousins in such anguish that only the sleep of utter exhaustion could stop the flow of their bitter tears.

It was Mariam who first succumbed to kind Nature, and Isabel, ever unselfish, found her one comfort in the sight of this slumber, uneasy though it was. She stole to the door and looked once more upon this weird, moon-flooded underworld. What she saw, however, reassured her. Not more than a dozen paces away was Black Eagle, standing like a statue, on guard. Suddenly that wild vista had no dread for her. Content, she closed the door, and soon she, too, was in the depths of slumber.

CHAPTER VI

IN THE DRAG NET

THE girls were aroused at midnight by loud shouts and the uproar of fierce conflict. The sounds of clashing weapons, the shrieks of the wounded, and the yells of the combatants made a rude awakening from the feeling of security with which they had at last fallen into slumber. Almost paralyzed with terror, Mariam and Isabel hurriedly arose and peered out, to see their new friends surrounded by a large force of warriors; to realize, too, that although fiercely resisting, Izon's party was being rapidly cut down. Merciless hand-to-hand fights were taking place all about them. They could see the tall forms of Izon and Black Eagle struggling desperately, side by side. One curious thing the onlookers noticed, even in all the excitement, that, while the most savage blows were showered on Black Eagle, none were directed toward Izon, the efforts of his assailants seeming to be to close in on him and capture him unharmed. Around him the fight was thickest.

IN THE DRAG NET

Izon and Black Eagle had been separated from their fellows in the rush, but now their own men strove madly to break through this cordon, and loud cries of "Strike for Izon!" resounded among them.

With sinking hearts Mariam and Isabel saw that their friends, far outnumbered, were being slowly but surely cut down. One of them who had been left to guard their hut, with the same cry for Izon upon his lips, stepped forward to meet a huge warrior who came rushing toward him and fell pierced through by the spear of his enemy. The slayer uttered a savage cry of victory in an unknown tongue, and the girls recognized this as a cry that, within the last few moments, had been growing general. Fiercer and fiercer grew the struggle, and just as they saw their defenders overwhelmed, the hut was burst open in the rear, they were seized, scarfs were thrown over their heads, and in this state they were carried a short distance, placed in some sort of conveyance, and borne away.

At first they could not comprehend what nature of vehicle they were in, but, after removing the scarfs, they felt about them in the darkness and decided that they were in a sort of litter or sedan chair which was being carried at a rapid pace. Overwhelmed by this new calamity they were at first numb with despair. Isabel, the more mercurial of the two, was the first to arouse to action, and she uttered one piercing scream after another, in the forlorn hope that, after all, their friends might rally and come to their assistance. Mariam thought at one time that she heard Black Eagle's distant shout in answer, but if there was such a response, it came only once, and silence answered all her other calls. Finding such efforts useless they gradually became calmer, encouraging each other to meet with fortitude whatever fate awaited them. Conversation was almost impossible, for they were subjected to the utmost discomfort, the roughness of the path causing their bearers to halt frequently and get assistance in the awkward places; but, after they had been jolted until they were almost exhausted, the pathway became smoother. Soon the bearers were moving more rapidly, with an easy jog which finally became so monotonous that it made the girls drowsy notwithstanding their anxiety. With this, sheer exhaustion had much to do, and in spite of all their efforts they slept. When they were awakened by the confusion attendant upon the

IN THE DRAG NET

change of bearers, they could tell by the rays of light which entered the crevices of the curtains around them that the sun had risen.

Suddenly other sounds besides the tramp of the bearers became apparent. The rattling of arms and what were evidently the challenges of sentinels were heard; they felt that their carriers were treading on paved streets, and the hum of a city grew unmistakable. The sounds became more pronounced as they advanced, until at last they were halted and the curtains drawn back. The brilliant light so dazzled their eyes that they could distinguish nothing. While they were still confused, a soldier addressed them in Spanish, requesting them to alight. They were cramped by their long confinement and could scarcely move, but when they did finally emerge from their litter, they found themselves surrounded by soldiers in the midst of a vast throng of strangely attired people who crowded about, gazing at them with curiosity, and uttering cries in an unknown tongue. The crowd filled a large plaza and the girls found themselves facing a huge palace-like structure built up against the cliff.

There was a roll of drums and fanfare of trumpets

PRINCE IZON

from a balcony above the entrance, and the attention of the concourse, except that of the guards, was momentarily diverted from the captives. Near them stood the officer in command of the guards. His face had a kindly expression as he turned to them with a reassuring smile. Suddenly he caught sight of the small cross which Isabel wore about her neck and he came nearer.

"I, too, am of the Faith," he said in a low tone in Spanish, pointing to the pendant. "Do not be afraid. I will find some way to protect you if possible."

"Oh, if you only can!" she replied earnestly. "Though I don't see why we should need protection. Where are we? Why were we brought here?"

"You are in the Red City, Ixtol, the people of which still worship Tezcatlipoca. I cannot tell you more now."

The trumpets and drums sounded, and captain and guards came to attention. A procession of brilliantly attired men and women issued from the portals of the palace and grouped themselves upon the flight of steps within the guard lines. An impressive silence fell as there appeared at the top of the stairway a remarkable looking man, with beard and eyes of black, who looked haughtily upon the assembled throng. His costume was superb. He was crowned with a head-dress composed of quetzal plumes, which, in the sunlight, had a sheen of golden green. A cloak made of turquoise blue feathers, woven upon cloth, reached from his shoulders to his feet; a golden belt encrusted with jewels circled his waist. His wrists and ankles were covered with golden bands, and his feet shod with golden sandals completed a costume which, for regal splendor, had not its like in the known world. His appearance, greeted by a final blare of trumpets, was the signal for instant prostration, and for loud cries in a language unknown to the girls, but which the captain interpreted for them into Spanish as "Hail, Topeltzin!" "Long live our high priest!"

He stood in stern dignity until silence ensued and then in a sonorous voice began a speech, which, as he spoke slowly, the captain was able to interpret phrase by phrase for his charges.

"Nobles, ladies, and people of great Ixtol. You know full well how many years your faithful priests have kept watch, ready at all times to serve our gods and you.

"This day, as many of you know, Tezcatlipoca comes to visit his realm for the first time in years.

"So greet him with all proper pomp. Let joy everywhere reign supreme, and while he deigns to be our guest, he must be paid all honor! I have spoken!"

The silence following his last words was broken by the sound of trumpets in the distance. A cry afar off and gaining volume as it raced toward them, at first a confused murmur and then a loud roar, was taken up by the multitude and turned into one savagely joyful shout, which the captain said was, "Tezcatlipoca comes! Hail to our god!"

The high priest suddenly caught sight of the little group of which the captives were the centre and beckoned to the captain. When he had approached, saluted, and reported, Topeltzin ordered him to bring them nearer. The fear that they evidently had of him seemed to please him, and at first they thought that he was going to address them. That, however, was not his way; turning to the crowd he called in a loud voice, and in the strange tongue, "Behold two strangers within our gates." Then to the girls in Spanish, "How came you here, and what is your country and your race, and what are your names?"

Mariam, though confused, preserved a calm exterior, and in as clear a voice as she could command told him that she and her friend were the daughter and niece of Don Ramon Navarez, formerly of Mexico, but of late years professor in a Western university in the States, that they were exploring the Grand Canyon where her father was lost in the river, and that they had come upon a party of men the day before who had promised them hospitality in a canyon city, but last night their party had been attacked and they had been carried away to this place. While she was speaking, Isabel noticed in the group surrounding Topeltzin, a beautiful young woman who had been observing them with evident vindictiveness. When Mariam ceased, this young woman spoke to Topeltzin.

"My lord, you know that our ancient laws decree swift death to strangers who witness the advent of our god, and the people are already clamoring that these laws be fulfilled."

In fact, the ominous murmurs were already increasing in the assemblage. Although the girls could not undertsand the language, the hostile meaning was only too plain, and they looked at each other in consternation. Turning instinctively for help from any quarter, Mariam saw the captain of the guards striding toward them with a look of pity. As he swiftly approached, thrusting back the crowd with his powerful arms, he made an almost imperceptible sign of the cross and as he drew near he reassured them in a low tone.

"Be brave! I will try to protect you."

Speechless with apprehension, they watched him as he commanded his men, who at once formed a circle of crossed spears between them and the crowd. The murmurs had now risen to an angry shout.

"What are they saying?" asked Mariam fearfully.

"Saying?" he grimly repeated. "They are yelling that their new god is coming and that you must die rather than see him. But some of them will never see him either if they try to harm you — stand back, you beast!" and with the butt of his spear the captain suddenly prodded in the breast a ferocious looking fellow who had been crouched as if for a spring through the cordon of guards. The man reeled back into the

IN THE DRAG NET

crowd deathly white, clutching at his crushed breast, and a laugh arose. It was an evidence of their bloodlust that they were able to make a jest of what proved to be a death blow. Horrified, the girls could only draw together and await the outcome. In the meantime the high priest and some of the nobles had gathered, and were apparently discussing the fate of the strangers, for frequent glances were cast in their direction.

"What a wicked expression that man has, Isabel!" whispered Mariam, catching the flashing eyes of Topeltzin fixed upon her.

"Wicked! He looks like wickedness itself!" replied Isabel. "What have we ever done to be led to this dreadful place? And there is no escape!"

"None, I am afraid," rejoined Mariam. "Our forefathers were warriors, let us remember, Isabel. We are only women, but we can die bravely."

A half-hysterical clutch upon Mariam's arm was Isabel's only answer. The shouting, fanatical crowd was now pressing closely around, and Topeltzin, motioning for silence, said to the girls in Spanish:

"Strangers, it is my painful duty to inform you that you must prepare for death. Our law decrees that any strangers who see our visiting god arrive in state, must die."

"Sir, you are not only inhospitable but wicked and unjust," replied Isabel, who, while she had not the calm courage of Mariam, had much more spirit. "We know nothing of your customs. We were told that we should receive a hospitable welcome in the canyon city, and as we have done no harm we demand that you let us go in peace."

As she spoke she noted his glowing black eyes dwelling upon Mariam, whose beauty was undimmed in spite of her recent hardships, and she thought that some pity might sway him. She was soon undeceived.

"I can do no more than to warn you to prepare for death. Tezcatlipoca even now approaches, and when he assumes dominion here, you must die."

The sentence of death from the autocrat spoken in Spanish and repeated in the other tongue, instantly communicated itself to the multitude, transforming their excitement into exultant rage, until the plaza resounded with the savage roar:

"Tezcatlipoca comes! Let them not offend his sight! Away with them! Kill them! Kill!"

CHAPTER VII

PRINCE IZON THE MIGHTY

THE mind of a crowd is as variable as the winds, shifting with every breeze, changing at a word, a nod, or even a telepathic impulse. The frenzied throng for whom Isabel and Mariam had been the centre of dangerous interest suddenly forgot them when the sound of approaching drums and trumpets was heard. A moment later the pomp of a glittering procession engrossed them, allowing the captain to lead the girls to a column near the middle of the plaza, where, still surrounded by the guards, they could see all that was taking place.

A passageway through the swaying concourse was opened by an advance band of drummers and Mariam and Isabel could not help noting that the instruments were the largest and finest they had ever seen, so numerous and so well played that the effect on the crowd was most inspiriting. Then came hundreds of flower girls, strewing the way with blossoms. The canyon

PRINCE IZON

echoed with triumphant shouts, which the multitude took up. To this succeeded, as the principal feature of the procession drew nigh, frantic choruses of cries in which the great name of Tezcatlipoca was the burden, and next appeared, following the flower girls, trumpeters heading a compact battalion of warriors. In their midst, standing on a platform that was carried upon the shoulders of twelve bearers, was a superb presence, glittering in the dazzling sunlight with hundreds of precious stones. Hardly in the hasheesh transported dreams of an Oriental potentate, could such a magnificent figure have been conjured up. The robes of the nobles and ladies surrounding Topeltzin, ornate as they were, now appeared almost tawdry by contrast, and even the high priest's superb trappings, that had seemed the extreme of all possible splendor, were cast into insignificance when compared to the gorgeous costume of this radiant being.

Thousands of tiny feathers, closely woven, formed a tunic in all the delicately blended colors of the prism. Golden sandals, bracelets, and belt, all studded with gems, sparkled with flashing rainbow tints. To crown the whole was a diadem of waving quetzal plumes, springing from a golden casque with visor-like beak, all in the most exquisitely chased fretwork.

Suddenly Isabel, turning from her contemplation of the costume itself to the one who wore it, clutched Mariam's arm in excitement.

"Izon!" she gasped.

But Mariam had already recognized him and was now standing in dumb amazement. Both of the girls were dazed. They could not reconcile the occurrence of yesterday with that of to-day. Yesterday, while Izon had been clad better than his fellows, still his raiment was rough and common; to-day he was robed in the most splendid costume that could be fashioned from all the treasures of a rich people. Only last night he had been attacked by a savage horde; to-day he was treated as a god. They were still more puzzled when Topeltzin gave a signal and all the great assemblage prostrated itself. The high priest also knelt and lifted up his hands.

"Mighty one, who condescends to honor us," he announced, "great lord of land and sea, behold us servile at your call! This palace is yours; this fair domain and all its subjects are at your command! To you, O Tezcatlipoca, we must humbly bow!"

A sonorous blare of the trumpets followed, when, in the midst of a tense silence, Izon spoke, his words ringing clear and firm:

"My people, I greet you again. I have come to reign over you once more: my country, that I love so dearly, my people that are all my own! Arise, my subjects!"

Turning, Izon for the first time noticed Mariam and Isabel, the only ones among those thousands still erect, and with a flush of relieved surprise he stretched forth his hand toward them.

"My dear friends," he called to them over the heads of the rising throng, "I welcome you as most honored guests beneath our roof. Welcome, thrice welcome, to our canyon home!"

Topeltzin looked up quickly with raised eyebrows, but he instantly waved his hand and the crowd fell back. The girls, bewildered by the unexpected turn of events, were conducted with the utmost respect to Izon.

"I am sorry," said he, bending down toward them

and smiling pleasantly, "that you should have been so inconvenienced. There has been a mistake made in our destination, that is all, but you shall have the hospitality I promised you." Turning to Topeltzin, he commanded,—"These ladies and the stranger who was taken with them are my own guests, and they must be housed with royal honors."

The chant was again taken up. The nobility on the stairway crowded back against the guards, forming a glittering lane. The flower girls passed up, strewing the way. Izon's litter was lowered to the ground, and, mounting the stairway, he was escorted into the palace with great ceremony.

The two girls were led in immediately after him, and were shown into a luxurious apartment. Advancing swiftly to meet them came the young woman who had incited the mob, but now she was quite different. Then she was jealous, now her face beamed with good will and courtesy. She kissed each upon her forehead and said in Spanish, with a slowness and precision that showed it was not her native tongue:

"I cannot express to you how deeply I regret having made so terrible a mistake. I hardly know how sufficiently to apologize and explain, but when you come, as you will, to understand the strange circumstances, and the explanation of Prince Izon, I am sure that you will forgive me."

Mariam and Isabel both gave her the assurance that courtesy demanded, and the young woman led them to couches where, reclining with them, she chatted long enough to put them at their ease. Her beauty was manifest. She gave her name as Zaliza, and told them she was the daughter of a great noble. She was an orphan who had been allowed to remain mentally a spoiled child, while attaining a superb physical development.

She could be tactful when she tried, however, for, seeing that the girls were weary, she clapped her hands, and a group of pretty attendants trooped in. Mariam and Isabel were led away, treated to a tepid bath, and supplied with fresh clothing from Zaliza's wardrobe. These garments were entirely different from their own, but the texture was so fine and the surfaces so soft and smooth that the effect upon their tired bodies was delightfully soothing. After being loosely robed they were conducted to another apartment where the light was almost entirely screened off, and they were left to rest upon downy couches.

After an hour's nap they were gently awakened and given some spiced hot broth, which was most invigorating. They were clad in outer garments and their hair dressed much in the style of Zaliza's, though the mode was varied to suit the coloring and facial contour of each. When they were led into the apartment where the Aztec girl had first received them and where she now awaited them, Zaliza herself gave an exclamation of delighted surprise at the transformation which had been wrought. Their new costumes were largely made up of the tiniest feathers, woven upon a background of cotton with a silk-like texture, a fabric so light and yet so firm, so warm and yet so beautiful, that no other textile could surpass it. In this canyon were birds of many species, including the sacred quetzal, some of which had been brought from Mexico, and bred in vast aviaries. The quetzal feathers were used by the nobility alone.

Isabel's rich brunette beauty was enhanced by dark red, while for Mariam the shimmering green that had

PRINCE IZON

been selected to match her Spanish blonde loveliness, made of her an indisputable queen in that palace where none but beauty was allowed to dwell. Presently Zaliza conducted them through a portion of the great building into the garden, and all eyes were turned upon the striking trio.

The visitors were too much occupied with wonder, which even intruded upon their sorrow, to notice the attention they were themselves attracting. The palace gardens which the Aztecs had constructed in Mexico were the marvels of their conquerors, but here in the Red City were all the improvements that centuries had made in artistic taste. Flowers spread masses of color harmony and fountains spouted high into the air, displaying rainbows in the bright sunshine.

This garden was only one of many that stretched back and up to the heights of the canyon, where the last towers of the palace reared toward the sky, and each garden differed from the others in its plan and decorative effect. Steps hewn in the rock and flanked by carvings led up from terrace to terrace, revealing constant surprises; yet varied as were these gardens, they were built with such consummate art that they still formed parts of one harmonious whole.

After the girls had revelled in this feast of beauty for some time, Isabel turned to Zaliza with a smile.

"We have been most delightfully misled," she said. "Prince Izon allowed us to understand that he was only an ordinary citizen. In spite of his modesty we surmised that he was of considerably more importance than he would have had us believe, but never could we have thought that he was the foremost man in the community, or that he could be the master of such a palace and such grounds."

"You were right in surmising the nobility of Prince Izon," replied Zaliza. "He is a direct descendant of Montezuma, hereditary ruler by right of blood of all the Aztecs. But on the other point you are mistaken. This palace does not belong to him, but to the high priest Topeltzin, who is really the autocrat of the Red City."

"But," interposed Mariam, "his word seemed law even to Topeltzin. Why, he was held as a god!"

"Yes — for a time," faltered Zaliza, changing color,

"and then —" she bit her lip to check back the words she was about to utter, and the girls could see that she had been on the point of revealing something about which she had been warned to say nothing.

Zaliza closed her eyes and shuddered after a moment of painful thought, then hastily excused herself, saying that she would be back in a few moments. Isabel gazed after her, surprised at her actions. To divert Mariam's mind from gloomy thoughts, she began to discuss the wonders they had seen. Noticing presently that silence only answered her, she turned to find Mariam gazing up the canyon with strained eyes and tense lips.

"What is the matter?" she exclaimed, and caught Mariam's clenched hands. They were deathly cold.

Mariam trembled and looked up with a start, as one awakening from a stupor.

"It is horrible!" she answered, speaking barely above a whisper and moistening her lips curiously. "Horrible! I think I know now why, when these marauders of the Red City captured Prince Izon, they were so careful not to harm him nor to place the slightest blemish upon his body. I think I know now why he

PRINCE IZON THE MIGHTY

was robed in the most costly garments that this rich people could furnish. I think I know now why he is held with such high honors and given the name of Tezcatlipoca, supreme god of the Aztecs. I think I know now why his word is law, why all this luxury and honor are his. 'For a time,' you remember Zaliza said. I have often heard my father speak of this anomalous treatment of certain captives. These are the exact conditions surrounding the unfortunates who are selected for the awful human sacrifices of the Aztecs. If this be true, our own fate at the end of this period is in but little doubt; and as for Izon, he is to die, and to die such a death that, oh!—" She covered her eyes with her hands and bowed her head in agony.

CHAPTER VIII
PLEASANT DAYS

ZALIZA, like a spoiled child, dreaded questioning, and adopted a subterfuge to avoid it. In place of returning, she sent, to divert their thoughts, a tall bronzed young man in fine Aztec garments. When he stood before them, it was Isabel who first recognized him.

"Black Eagle!" she cried. "How came you here, and in that costume?"

"In a moment," he replied. "First tell me of Izon; is he safe?"

"Why,— have you not seen him? Do you not know?"

"I know nothing except my own experience," replied the chieftain. "The last I saw of Izon was in the fight last night, when he was surrounded and bound by a crowd of our assailants. I had caught sight of the party that was carrying you off and tried to follow, calling to you. So many were against me that I thought as

I could not help you then, I might do so later, so I threw up my hands. Instead of spearing me they tied me and led me to this strange place. They put me in a cave in the cliffs under guard, but a short time ago they led me out, bowed before me, gave me food and wine and these clothes, and at last conducted me here. But tell me about Izon. I am going to be discourteous enough to let you keep your own story for the last, because I see you are safe."

Briefly Isabel related all, and with deep anxiety Mariam told her surmises about Izon's fate. Black Eagle had risen to his feet during this recital, and now, stretching his brawny arms, he said, smiling,

"For some time, you tell me? Then we have nothing to fear. I do not think that this place can hold Izon and myself any longer than we desire."

His confidence was reassuring, and the girls quickly shared it, but they decided to say nothing to Izon about this for the present. Presently Zaliza entered with Izon, and, no sooner were the four reunited, than anxiety vanished. The two men seemed so strong and so capable, and they appeared so confident of safety, that dark forebodings could have no place now in the minds of any of them. They had been so thrown together by trials that they seemed to be of a united family, with the exception of Zaliza. The Aztec beauty contrived at last to divert them from their reunion, and, manœuvring so that she secured Izon as her escort, led the way to the upper garden.

Emerging upon the terrace, the party was treated to one of the most magnificent views with which the human mind could be enthralled. The sublimity of the canyon as seen from the upper plateau, here took a new and most enchanting aspect. They were now midway down the abyss, and as far as the eye could see, there were pyramids and castles and temples and precipices in stupendous grandeur, all glowing in a riot of variegated and brilliant colors that constantly changed into new and exquisite combinations as the sunlight was occasionally shaded by the billows of rolling clouds, enveloping some of the mighty peaks.

Below them and sweeping around the bends of the cliff, spread out upon a large mesa, was the Red City itself, a succession of houses, streets and gardens and several plazas. The red granite that had given the city

PLEASANT DAYS

its name was seen everywhere, but in a variety of harmoniously blended shades.

The streets were alive with movement and color. There were soldiers uniformed in flashing tabards, and marching to the cadence of their splendid drums; priests, in slow procession, garbed in sombre gray; jugglers and tumblers performing wonderful feats; bearers, in files with high packs; merchants, in groups, each one costumed in flowing robes; nobles, distinguished by tossing quetzal plumes set in jewelled turbans, each noble attended by a retinue of servants; Aztec ladies, passing in and out of the markets, or bending over the tempting wares of the open-fronted shops; merry children running about or playing in the waters of the many fountains, their shrill cries mingling with the deeper sounds of the multitude; litters, from which bright eyes peered out through delicate canopies. Weaving through the moving throng were goats bearing panniers or pulling carts filled with their own contributions to all this teeming life,— with milk and cream and cheese, with tender kid flesh and dried meats, with wool and skin, and hides for tanning, with horns and bone and glue and other by-products. And they saw the large bronze turkeys which were, even in the day of Cortez, the principal food of the Aztecs. The whole panorama was one of unending interest and picturesqueness, variety and vivacity.

This was but the beginning of many days of gay entertainment, which while it did not annul the sorrow of Mariam or Isabel, at least kept them from falling into melancholy. A party of young people were waiting for them at the palace. They were the sons and daughters of nobles who had been appointed by Topeltzin as attendants to Izon and his guests, and they prized the honor highly. Though Zaliza and the other maids of honor and the young men who had been appointed in the train of Izon, lived in the palace of the high priest for the time being, they had fine homes in the city, and in these Izon and his guests were welcomed and treated with every luxury.

Provided with turkey quills filled with grain gold which formed the Aztec money, they shopped in the quaint market place; they visited the quarters of the metal workers and of the feather weavers where they saw such gold work and textiles as have never been sur-

PLEASANT DAYS passed. They were taken to the drift where gold was extracted by dredging in such quantities that it was put to common uses — even for kitchen utensils. They took trips through the city; but their favorite resting place was the upper terrace of the palace garden.

One morning Black Eagle and the two girls were alone in this garden. They were discussing anew the tragedy of the canyon, when a faint sound, a peculiar, long-drawn yodel came to their ears. To the girls it meant nothing, but to Black Eagle it evidently had some intensely exciting import. He examined the surface of the cliff minutely. It towered full ninety feet straight up, an apparently unscalable height. There did, it is true, run from the top to the bottom a slight diagonal seam, and this seam Black Eagle carefully examined. There came a repetition of the strange call. He slipped off his sandals, and turned to his companions.

"Good-bye," he said, "I have heard a command so incredible that I do not dare conjecture. I can only obey."

They could not conceive what he meant. It looked impossible for any creature without wings to scale the height, but they were astounded to see Black Eagle attempt it. Clinging to the inequalities of the surface with fingers and toes, and following the fissure, he crept slowly upward, inch by inch, foot by foot, until he was half-way up the face of the precipice and the girls with bated breath, clenched hands, and straining eyes stood in horrified expectation of seeing him fall to be crushed. Suddenly a man rushed past them and began to climb the same crevice which the chieftain had used. They recognized him as a stalwart Aztec priest whom they had seen flitting about and who was in reality one of Topeltzin's spies to watch their every movement. He had been concealed behind a projecting ledge all the while, and, seeing Black Eagle about to escape and knowing that a death by torture awaited him if he did not prevent it, he rushed up in a frenzy and began to scale the cliff in pursuit of the chieftain. Stifled screams from the girls gave Black Eagle warning. Looking down, he instantly comprehended the situation and called to the girls in Spanish, "Don't be alarmed. I will manage him."

The peaceful scene which had existed only a few moments before was now changed to one of tragic excitement, although all the actors were silent, as the in-

PLEASANT DAYS

terest of each demanded no discovery of the situation. The Aztec like the Indian had bared his feet and, being of athletic build, rapidly caught up with Black Eagle, who had ceased climbing and was busied in securing a foothold and in bracing himself. Slowly the priest crept near enough to grasp for the chieftain's foot. Isabel expected to see Black Eagle kick him down, but he did not. Instead, he drew up his feet, forcing the Aztec to climb higher. As he made another effort to clutch the chieftain, the latter, holding to a crevice with his left hand, suddenly bent down and with his right hand seized the Aztec by the collar of his tunic and jerked him away from the cliff. Both girls shuddered as they saw Black Eagle swing his captive back and forth, Isabel recalling the story he had told her at the brink of the canyon, and they crouched against the cliff. Mariam covered her eyes from the sight to come, but Isabel stared with fascinated gaze as the swings grew longer.

CHAPTER IX

TOPELTZIN OUTLINES HIS PLOT

THE private rooms of Topeltzin were most luxurious, but one room was an exception; and today he occupied this apartment. Although Topeltzin was a voluptuary of monstrous desires, there was an austerity about his mental processes that made him the greatest man of his own domain. There were no luxuries here where he stood brooding, looking out of the window to the opposite canyon wall. He had risen to be autocrat of the Red City not by inheritance, as the position was elective, but by sheer force of character. It is true that ominous whispers had been circulated at the time concerning the mysterious deaths of two of his rivals, but the whispers had soon ceased owing to the awe in which he was held through the swift punishment meted out to any one who dared oppose him. Presently he turned impatiently from the window and began to pace the floor, counting his steps mechanically, fourteen paces forward, fourteen paces backward.

TOPELTZIN OUTLINES PLOT

"By Tezcat!" he cried presently, and then summoned a servant.

"Zeno!" the master commanded.

In a few moments a youthful Aztec priest entered and bowed profoundly.

"Be seated," said Topeltzin. Such politeness on occasions to an inferior is one of the characteristics of the great.

"May Huitzilopochtle, Lord of the Universe, forever guard you, my lord."

"No, Zeno, my 'patron saint,' as the Christians say, is Tezcatlipoca, he of eternal youth; invoke him for me rather than the ancient Huitzilopochtle."

As he spoke, Topeltzin turned to the window and looked gloomily out across the canyon, but soon he wheeled impatiently.

"Zeno," he said, "did you ever hear of angels?"

Zeno smiled.

"Those beautiful beings whom the Christians say live in their heaven and sometimes visit the earth, my lord?"

"The same!" agreed Topeltzin. "If ever one of these creatures has assumed the shape of a woman it certainly must be this Mariam. Our gods themselves surely cannot have lovelier consorts. Her companion, Isabel, is almost as beautiful and more vivacious, so I think I shall acquire the two. But, my good Zeno, here precisely is the complication. After waiting so many years to catch the cursed Christians of the upper city napping, and after at length capturing their greatest prize, it will not do to make a blunder. Izon has made these two girls and the Indian his 'honored guests.' His commands, even to me, must be law, and he knows this as well as I do. There, then, is my problem. I have spent two or three days searching for a solution to it, and have not seen a satisfactory one as yet. So, my good Zeno, you who have helped me in so many intrigues, both of state and person, I turn the matter over to you as food for thought."

"I accept the task, my lord," replied Zeno. "It should not be one of so much difficulty. It would seem to me only to be necessary to turn Izon from his present wooing of this Mariam."

"So!" exclaimed the high priest, frowning. "It has begun, has it? I had thought so from the first. 'Tis the way of the gods. Your plan is probably right.

TOPELTZIN OUTLINES PLOT

What have been the movements of our 'guests' up to the present?"

"The movements of any frivolous young people who have nothing to do but to amuse themselves, my lord," replied Zeno. "They have been seeing the city, tasting of all its amusements and pleasures."

"And Izon? He bears himself smilingly then, through it all?"

"My lord, we expected nothing else from a son of the Montezumas. He is apparently the most care-free of them all, and the people adore him. Tezcatlipoca never had a more perfect representative, and he is hailed as the veritable god."

Topeltzin sneered. "This Mariam, then, and Izon smile and sigh upon each other, do they? Well, let not one smile nor sigh escape the eyes of your secret force, and, by Tezcat! we shall see if we cannot divert them."

Zeno's face flushed.

"I fear that this can be done but too easily," he said, biting his lip.

"Indeed? What do you mean?"

"That Zaliza is infatuated with him; so much so that she has given a hint to me, me! my lord! that she will petition you to appoint her one of the three to share his last revels."

For a moment Topeltzin looked blankly amazed and then he chuckled.

"Why, this falls out as it should! Tezcatlipoca is aiding me!" he exulted. "We must encourage this!"

Zeno looked up at him piteously, but the high priest scorned him. "So, my good Zeno, you will persist in having emotions of your own!"

"I cannot help it, my lord!" groaned Zeno. "In spite of everything, I am still a man, and have within me some of the attributes of a god, and there are times when I would wield thunder-bolts!" and his eyes blazed with sudden fierceness.

"It is a fatal longing, that, Zeno," counselled Topeltzin dryly, "and I advise you to cast it out of your mind. If there are any thunder-bolts to be wielded here, I shall hurl them, as I represent the powers. In the meantime I want to know more of this affair of your pretty Zaliza. By the Gods, what a vixen she is! What does Izon seem to think of her?"

"My lord, he makes no secret of his love for

TOPELTZIN OUTLINES PLOT

Mariam. It is mutual, though I doubt if the maid realizes it as yet. It can be seen by all, however. As for Zaliza, she has eyes for the prince alone. She is jealous enough of Mariam to do her any mischief. Yet she feigns friendship for both the girls. She does so, I am certain, only that she may be near them to watch their every action and to torture herself with each glance that Izon bestows upon this golden-haired stranger. Me, she scorns! Your pardon, my lord! I am no longer a man when I think how she jeers and spurns me, and oh, my great chief, use your mighty power, I beg you! Let me find another way to influence Izon, and Zaliza will have but myself to consider! But one word from you — "

"Enough!" said Topeltzin sternly. "You shame Tezcatlipoca as my foremost pupil! The woman is there; you have access to her. If you cannot win her you should scorn to have her forced! Come to me with no more of your whining. Observe, I bid you, my methods in affairs of this sort. Here, for instance, like two birds into a snare, have these two girls fluttered into my hands. Shall I close the snare and crush the birds, or shall I teach them to warble sweetly in their cages? Ah, there is no music like the song of an unwilling bird that has been tamed to docility."

Topeltzin laughed while Zeno shuddered at the diabolical ring.

"My lord, all power and wisdom abide in you," he replied humbly. "Order, and I will obey."

"Continue your work as I have outlined it," commanded the high priest. "Remember this as though coming from the gods themselves. For your own affair, let me give you advice that will hold good in all similar cases. Use the dark Spanish girl, Isabel, as a means to influence Zaliza. Jealousy is a weapon that seldom fails. Here, I will give you a more detailed thought," and in a whisper, seemingly fearful of even the walls, he rapidly outlined a plan that made Zeno's face light up with a singular expression of mingled satisfaction and vindictiveness.

"May Tezcatlipoca forever guard you, my lord," he said as he withdrew, bowing profoundly and backing through the doorway.

Topeltzin looked once more across the canyon but

TOPELTZIN OUTLINES PLOT

his face was no longer gloomy. Instead, he stroked his beard and smiled grimly at the landscape which only minutes before had held for him but troubled visions.

"O Tezcatlipoca, Lord of Eternal Youth," he said, turning to a golden image of the deity on a pedestal in a corner of the room, "behold the service I will do in your honor. These men and women will now move at my will all to one great end, the consummation of the sacrifice in your honor, and giving me as your servant a triple satisfaction that no other human being will ever have enjoyed, vengeance and power and pleasure. First, overwhelming victory over Zolcoma whom I hate, over the Christian God upon whom I spit! Second, the subjugation or the death of Izon which will give me supreme power over both cities. And third, and grandest of all, the possession of these proud beauties!"

A light drumming at the tympanum of his speaking tube arrested his attention, and with a frown he bent over it. The modern Aztecs, but little behind the rest of the world in civilization, had not yet found electricity; in place of it they had wonderfully developed hydraulics and pneumatics. Tubes connected drum to drum, and vibrated to a central station where the commands of an imperious master and of his court received instant attention.

The message that came to him consisted of but half a dozen words, but they were enough to make him furious. Zeno again appeared before him in answer to his command.

"I have just learned," he said in a whisper of rage, "that Black Eagle is nowhere to be found! I gave you orders that not one of the four were to be from under your watch!"

"My lord, I do not know how it could have happened," stammered Zeno.

"What matters how it happened! The fact is that it did, and that you are responsible! Come here! By Tezcat! you shall feel his rage."

Zeno obeyed, trembling. Topeltzin suddenly grasped him around the throat. He was a powerful man and was terrible in anger. It was only that he still had need of Zeno that he spared him, and when he had vented his anger he threw the insensible youth from him and left the apartment, where some priests, Zeno's assistants in the department of espionage, sat with livid faces. With

TOPELTZIN OUTLINES PLOT

a calmness that they feared more than his violence, he drew from them all that they knew. The two girls and Black Eagle had been on the upper terrace, watched by their comrade Mazan. Only the girls had come down. The men surely could not have climbed the cliff. The grounds and the palace had been well searched before the matter had been reported to Topeltzin. It was impossible for Black Eagle or Mazan to have escaped. Nevertheless they were gone, and the only ones who could explain it were Izon, Mariam, or Isabel, and they said nothing.

"And they will not, for I shall not ask them!" said Topeltzin grimly. "I dare not, lest it defeat our own ends, by displaying our purpose through our anxiety. I suppose you craven incompetents remember the tradition, that when strangers once more descend upon us and leave our domain alive, great Ixtol shall be no more. And would you know what is likely to happen to each of you if Black Eagle is not quickly found? Then go and look after your captain Zeno, and let him tell you, if he is able to speak. Beware of my punishment, for it shall be that of our avenging gods!"

CHAPTER X

THE VOICE FROM THE PLATEAU

MARIAM, not hearing the expected crash of the falling Aztec priest, opened her eyes to see Isabel staring up with an expression of amazement. Following her gaze, she was equally astonished to see the two men slowly climbing the cliff, the Aztec in advance. Isabel could explain but little. Black Eagle had said something to the priest, who had answered, and then the chieftain had swung him back to the seam in the cliff, and together they had begun the ascent.

After a breathless time for the girls, the men gained the top, and Black Eagle, waving a farewell to them and repeating the yodel call, disappeared with his companion.

The two men found themselves upon a rugged plateau, the impassability of which explained why the Aztecs had located below. It was a maze of great rocks that lay strewn in wild confusion, as if some lake of stone had been upheaved, and tossing its jagged frag-

VOICE FROM THE PLATEAU

ments in every direction, had been left a chaos — was like a petrified ocean storm. Still beyond, arose the spine of a tortuous mountain range, so that to white man and to Indian alike, an impassable barrier was apparently presented. Yet, men had trodden it, for just below them were half a dozen soldiers and two white-haired men. One of these had great difficulty in suppressing his emotions as, looking up, he saw the tall form of Black Eagle silhouetted against the sky. It was Professor Raymon!

Black Eagle, in spite of the peculiar call which had been adopted by the professor and himself as a distress signal, could scarcely believe his eyes. It was enough for him that the call had sounded. He would have tried to arise from his death bed to obey that summons. He had firmly believed the professor was dead; but he answered and followed willingly, even though the voice had come from beyond the grave.

Now that he saw Professor Raymon alive, he joyfully waved his hand in salute; but to join him found he had to jump down about twenty feet to a narrow ledge, below which yawned a crevasse of fearful depth. He nearly toppled over backwards as he landed, but caught himself by a herculean effort. For a period of breathless suspense he crouched, poised upon the very edge of the ledge. Every muscle was tense and quivering. He put forth all his efforts to force the centre of gravity upon the safe side. The tendons of his lower limbs stood out like knotted cables. Inch by inch he forced his bulk forward, and a shout of joy went up from below when finally he was able to throw himself forward upon the ledge, there to lie panting. His breath recovered, it was an easy matter for him to steady the priest when he dropped and to pick his way around to the party where he was eagerly awaited.

"My daughter and Isabel?" cried Professor Raymon.

"They are safe and well, but grieving for you."

"And Prince Izon?" quickly inquired the other white-haired man, whom Professor Raymon introduced as Father Zolcoma, of the Pearl City.

"Safe and well and brave," replied Black Eagle.

"Let us give thanks," said the venerable priest, and amidst the kneeling circle he offered up a heartfelt prayer of gratitude.

In telling each one's story, Professor Raymon

VOICE FROM THE PLATEAU

naturally came first, as of one risen from the dead. His escape from the cataract had been almost miraculous. Going over the fall he had been sucked beneath the rapids. Their swirl drew him down, then threw him to the surface, and he was shot with great velocity upon the top of the current to where, at a sharp curve in the bank, he was cast under the shelter of a rock, and jammed into a wedge-like opening. Here, bruised and stunned, he had lain for how long he could not tell, except that when he finally regained consciousness he was faint from both hunger and pain. Doubtless the girls in their frantic search for him had passed and repassed a few feet above him. When he was able to move he crawled to the trail above, where he was picked up by the patrol that had been left behind by Prince Izon to search for his body. They, following behind as they did, escaped the sortie of the Red City band, and the attendant massacre. When they came upon the spot, however, they found fearful evidences of what had happened, and hurried on to the White City as rapidly as the dangerous condition of the professor would permit. Ever since, Father Zolcoma and others of Prince Izon's intimate connections had been trying to glean news of the status of their beloved ruler, and now that they knew him to be safe for the present, they were overjoyed.

"It is only for a short time, I fear, however," said Black Eagle, resuming his narrative. "From the royal treatment they are according him and from some strange remarks which I overheard, I think that Prince Izon has been set aside for sacrifice."

"They would not dare!" hastily interposed Professor Raymon. "Why, I am told that he is the sixteenth in direct line of descent from Montezuma!"

"Dare!" exclaimed Father Zolcoma. "They would dare anything, these wicked pagans over whom Topeltzin reigns; and it is the plot of that crafty high priest to kill off all the royal blood of the Aztecs but his own line, thus being in a position to rule both cities."

"Are there no men then in your Pearl City?" demanded Black Eagle sharply. "Are there no warriors, that they stand idle while their prince is in such danger?"

"Gently, brother," replied Father Zolcoma. "There are none but sturdy men in the Pearl City. They have

VOICE FROM THE PLATEAU

not been softened and enervated by the deadly vices that hold those of the Red City within their grip. But there is a most weighty reason why the plan you suggest is not feasible. It is that the moment armed forces were to break in upon the Red City, Izon would die. No man set aside for the obsidian sacrifice may ever be rescued alive."

Professor Raymon turned pale.

"And most likely, those captured with him must die too," he said. "No, Black Eagle, there must be some other way. Cannot Prince Izon and the girls come out by the same path you scaled?"

"No woman can do it," replied Black Eagle, "although there are many in the Havasupai tribe that could accomplish it. Even if there were a chance for Prince Izon there would be none for the girls."

"And if he were to escape, leaving them behind," interrupted Professor Raymon, "I shudder to conjecture their fate."

"Nothing of the sort will be done," Black Eagle calmly returned. "We will all four of us get away, or none of us."

"Do you mean to say that you are going back, after

having once escaped their clutches?" asked Father Zolcoma.

"Of course."

Professor Raymon fondly put his hand upon Black Eagle's shoulder.

"He is my blood-brother, my sworn blood-brother," he explained.

"Yes, while life shall last!" added Black Eagle. "But even if I had not been, there is that within Prince Izon, your daughter, and your niece, any one and all of them, that would command loyalty to the death. I am going back, and there will be four of us to die or four to escape. If we do die we shall not die alone. We shall have many Aztec priests and warriors as our servants in the land of shades."

"Who is that man?" asked Professor Raymon, pointing to the Aztec priest who had been standing at a distance in an attitude of dejection.

Black Eagle briefly explained.

"When I had him in my power," he continued, "I realized that if I dropped him he would live long enough to explain my escape, so I told him he had better climb up with me and go to the Pearl City, where he would not be harmed. Between the alternative of my offer or of being crushed to death, or of being tortured to death by Topeltzin, he chose the former."

The party now rose and took up their march towards the Pearl City. In the direction they were travelling the way seemed more impassable than ever. In fact, Black Eagle could not see how they were to surmount the forbidding obstacles that lay before them. They had clambered over but two or three of the impediments, however, when, instead of attempting to scale the next one, the foremost of the party let himself down into a hole formed beneath two slabs. Such apertures were common in this chaos of boulders, strewn apparently by Titans at play, and Black Eagle could not have distinguished this one from any other of its kind. Nevertheless, when it came his turn to descend, he did so; letting go boldly as he had seen the others do, and dropping into a dark pocket scarcely higher than his head.

Those in advance of him had already moved on, and following them cautiously he went down two or three uneven steps and found himself in a natural fissure-like tunnel.

PRINCE IZON

For nearly an hour they travelled this underground runway that had been formed by some upheaval of nature. They walked in single file, each grasping a cord that passed from the leader down the line. Daylight finally appeared in the distance, and when at last Black Eagle emerged, he gave a cry of amazement. Before him the canyon widened out, the two vast arms of a circle stretching in both directions; below him rolled the river; there was a tremendous roar of a distant waterfall in his ears; everywhere the cliffs were of pearly whiteness and there, just before him, arose from the winding mesa, the buildings, palaces, and majestic temple of the Pearl City!

CHAPTER XI

LUXTOL, THE PEARL CITY

GOTHIC architecture is man's aspiration toward heaven, frozen into stone. Gothic in white is that aspiration purified and spiritualized. Such was the Pearl City. An old cathedral engraving, in the possession of a Spanish priest who had fled from Mexico with the Aztecs, had been the inspiration for all the structures in the Christian colony of the canyon. Its principles had been seized upon with avidity by these skilled workers of stone, and out of the white quartz and marble which abounded there, they had wrought a veritable elysium. Flying buttresses of graceful proportions shot down the steep sides of the mesa wherever its projections afforded a solid footing, and strengthened noble piles of architecture that swept upward from arch to arch until they terminated in lofty pinnacles, pointing the thoughts of men ever upward.

As Black Eagle and his companions skirted the outer rim of this tremendous natural amphitheatre, the ledge they were traversing grew broader and led upwards toward a distant white marble bridge which swept across from cliff to mesa. The parapet of the ledge grew gradually more ornate, and new beauties were revealed at every turn. Every edifice was imposing, for in building the Pearl City no small structure had been planned, life here being communal, so that under the roof of each dwelling at least a score of families were housed, much as in the modern apartment buildings. By this plan of working with large units it was possible to design a city which should be harmonious throughout, and no architectual view in the world could surpass the one that lined this mesa front — an elongated ellipse.

Gradually becoming accustomed to the increasing beauty of the scene, Black Eagle thought that he had lost his ability to marvel further, but when he had stepped at last upon the bridge, he gave a gasp of astonishment, for, in the centre of the city there confronted him a church of white marble, superb with all that gold and skill and devotion could lavish. A wide avenue led up to it, and this avenue was bordered by stately pillars, each bearing a sculptured figure. The temple itself presented a broad façade, flanked by noble towers with

LUXTOL, THE PEARL CITY

spires of gold, and this façade was repeated upon the four points of the compass, the whole comprising a Greek cross in ground plan. Flying arches supported a lofty dome, from which, by receding buttressed stories, reared on high the tower that bore in upper air the golden cross which had been seen from afar in the mirage.

As the little party drew near the church, the sound of approaching music was heard, and presently a long procession in solemn chant appeared upon the great plaza and began filing slowly in at the doorway. The chant swelled in sonorous cadence as the singers marched on, and Black Eagle turned to Professor Raymon inquiringly.

"It is a procession for the safety of Prince Izon," the professor explained. "Every day, for a week, this ceremony has been held. The procession you see is but one of the four that are now entering simultaneously at the four façades, and several thousand people are taking part in it. Other thousands will take it up to-morrow and others the next day, while on Sunday the entire population will join in the supplication. Can such devotion go unrewarded?" The eyes of Professor Raymon were moist as he spoke, and as Black Eagle was silent because of emotion, the professor laid a hand upon his shoulder and continued: "My brother, after all these years, I have found what I never expected in my life to see, a whole city where there is no wickedness and no poverty, where every one fears God and obeys Him; and I desire nothing more than to gather my own loved ones close around me and spend my declining years in this place."

They stood with bared heads until the procession had all been swallowed up within the doorway, when they, too, followed. Large as was the throng, it seemed quite small when housed under that lofty dome which, resting upon its graceful arches, seemed floating in mid air, that curved upward and inward until its blue tinting, merging into the dimness of the apex, seemed to blend into a lovely twilight sky. The soft light, streaming down from the drum of the dome, from the four rose windows and from the clear story, touched with a radiant glow the double row of columns, bringing out their delicate tracery. It cast the long aisles into restful half shadows; it bathed in effulgence the beautiful altar

LUXTOL, THE PEARL CITY

of marble and gold, and it rested upon the heads of the kneeling congregation like a benediction.

Black Eagle had scarcely time to comprehend these things when a low, deep chord of wondrous sweetness stole upon his ears, starting softly as the trembling sighs of distant æolian harps, and gradually swelling, the sonorous strains filled the edifice with their glorious harmonies that sent thrills of ecstatic emotion to the hearts of the hearers. Other and higher chords joined in, and then, throughout the building, resounded the notes of a solemn Sanctus, played upon an immense water organ, the pipes of which occupied an entire façade. It was the noblest music that the Havasupai chieftain had ever heard, and it melted him to tears. Had he not long since become a convert to the teachings of one of the intrepid Western missionaries, his heart would have been awed and subjugated under that wonderful flood of melody.

Upon the conclusion of the services Black Eagle left the cathedral with the exalted mind of one who has been nearer to his Maker. Father Zolcoma and Professor Raymon were in earnest converse just behind him with several dignified looking men, and outside, upon the steps, a second priest joined them. Black Eagle, seeing that they were intensely interested, walked slowly around the plaza, studying this marvellous new city and its people. He was surprised to note that the inhabitants, while obviously Aztec, were more intelligent looking than the people of the other city. Nowhere could he see the coarse faces that were so prevalent in the Red City, but in their places were the clear eyes, the clean, firm cheeks of those who live righteously and think honestly. As for the city itself, he found that the streets radiated in every direction from the temple, which was in the centre of the city, the cross streets being concentric with the ellipse of the mesa. The inner circle was occupied by shops, and on the streets back of this began apartment houses, while each circle farther back gave place to higher buildings with more ornate sky lines, each street ending in the mesa brink against some palace and presenting a splendid vista at both ends. The avenues leading straight out from the four façades gave views across the canyon, on the two sides opening upon wide bridges, but on the end facing the head of the canyon the avenue was stopped by a pierced parapet,

LUXTOL, THE PEARL CITY

and beyond glittered and flashed in the sunlight the waterfall, that, pouring down its thunderous, mist-shrouded flood, gave to the city not only its water supply but its characteristic undertone and its most beautiful vista. It was a perpetual glory, like the covenant of the rainbow, and a constant reminder to the people of the Pearl City that behind all their destinies was an all-powerful Being to whom no task was too great for accomplishment.

Black Eagle had completed the circle of the plaza and was re-approaching Father Zolcoma's group when Professor Raymon, seeing him, called him to them. He introduced him to Lord Toltec, as the uncle of Prince Izon, and to the other dignitaries, then to Father Orlozo.

"We have been waiting for you," said Father Zolcoma. "We have a plan by which we think the release of Prince Izon and his companions may possibly be effected. Come, and we will discuss it."

The party walked slowly out to a palace which blocked one of the radial streets. Black Eagle was prepared, from the artistic work that had been put upon its exterior, to find the interior of equal richness, but upon entering he was at once struck by the startling contrast between the severity of the furnishings of these apartments and the luxury of those in the palace of Topeltzin. It was in itself an index to the differing aims and purposes in life of the two dignitaries. The apartments were large and well lighted, and while all the furniture and fittings were in harmony with the building itself, there was an utter absence of all pandering to mere comfort and ease.

Black Eagle had at first supposed that this palace was devoted to the use of Father Zolcoma and his immediate household. He found, however, that here dwelt all the priesthood of the Pearl City, and when the party had passed to an upper floor, he noted a succession of small white rooms, plainly furnished.

"I presume these are for the acolytes and minor priests," Black Eagle ventured to Lord Toltec, with whom he was talking.

"They are for all the priests," replied the venerable man. "This one we have just passed is Father Orlozo's, and this one is Father Zolcoma's," and they entered and took seats around a centre table.

The room was exactly like the others, no better and

no different in any way. A new light dawned upon the visitor and in his inner consciousness he knew that ultimately the Pearl City must win against the Red. The victories of all the world have been won by those who disdained bodily ease. A born leader of men, Father Zolcoma was easily accorded the precedence by the aged Lord Toltec, and the other elders, in the consultation that ensued, although he sought and obtained their approval in all such matters before acting.

"My son," said he, addressing Black Eagle, "and you too, my brother," he added, turning to Professor Raymon, "I am going to tell you a secret known to but very few. You remember the crevasse and the tunnel by which you reached our portion of the canyon?"

Black Eagle nodded.

"Well, in the end of that crevasse nearest the Red City, relays of workmen are tunnelling cautiously into the solid rock, with the purpose of effecting a secret entrance through one of the grottos in Topeltzin's garden. We cannot tell as yet which grotto we shall strike, and I want you and your companions to spend as much time as possible in the garden in order to find out which one we are approaching. We shall leave at least a foot of rock between our tunnel and the wall. We will let you know when we are ready. Your task will be to secrete yourselves in the grotto that night alone, if possible, so that when we break through, you can be ready to slip into the cut. As soon as all four of you are safe it has been arranged that the entrance will be blocked, and from that moment danger is past. It is simply a matter of walking through the crevasse to its mouth, where you emerged to-day."

"And once within our gates," said Lord Toltec, earnestly. "A royal welcome will be tendered your friends and yourself with the ovation to Izon."

At this juncture there was a knock on the door. At Father Zolcoma's invitation to come in a young priest entered, his eyes sparkling and his cheeks flushed with excitement.

"We have found it!" he cried. "We know now how it is possible for Topeltzin to keep informed daily of all our movements. It is the most remarkable development of a mysterious natural gift that we have discovered. Come with me and I will show you Topeltzin's greatest achievement."

LUXTOL, THE PEARL CITY

"Where is this?" asked Father Zolcoma, rising.

"In our own palace," the young man replied.

"And Topeltzin's agent?" asked Father Zolcoma.

"One of your own converts!"

CHAPTER XII
LOVE'S TELEGRAPH

A HOUSE that abounds in secret passages has a master whose mind abounds in dark byways. It was noted of Topeltzin that he appeared and disappeared in the most unexpected places about his palace, the elements of surprise always attending him. Into one of these hidden corridors he turned shortly after the discovery of Black Eagle's disappearance, emerging into a concealed room which was most peculiarly furnished. Its walls and ceiling were hung in a black, velvet-like fabric, a frieze of gold fretwork and a gold centre panel in the ceiling being their only relief. The carpet, too, was of black. A couch and chair, also in black, were the only articles of furniture, except a small table upon which reposed the fragments of a half-eaten meal. Only one window lighted the room, and this, from the depth of its embrasure, was through a very thick wall.

LOVE'S TELEGRAPH

The most striking object in the room, however, was a young girl dressed in black. Her hair also was of raven hue so that her face, of waxen fairness, was the only object which the light could throw into relief, and when she moved within the Stygian environment her countenance seemed to be afloat within that living sepulchre, with a spectral effect that would have been startling to one who might have come upon it unaware. Just now, however, she was seated at her table before the window, gazing steadfastly out upon a view that was comprised of nothing but a far-distant golden cross, blazing in the afternoon sun against a background of blue sky and drifting white clouds. She did not turn as Topeltzin came into the apartment; she did not hear him. Her elbows were resting upon the table, the fingers of each hand pressed upon her temples and the palms upon her cheeks, thus supporting her head. Her eyes seemed to look beyond the cross to some other view which filled her mental vision to the exclusion of all else. She seemed rapt and strained in her attention, and Topeltzin, without making any attempt to conceal or muffle his movements, strode over to the couch and sat down upon it where he could watch her face. She was talking in a low, musical voice, and he listened to her attentively.

"Ah, my beloved!" she was saying. "Where have you been? For more than an hour I have lost you. Across the cruel space that has mocked us since the morning of our nuptial day, I have been sending forth my soul to you, calling, calling, all in vain, and your spirit has not answered me. Only now have I felt your presence again. I think that in another hour I would have swooned. Oh, my husband, speak to me! Tell me again of your love and that it shall last until this weary torture of probation is over! — Yes, life of my soul, I hear you."

She ceased to speak. She intensified her gaze, and with half parted lips seemed to be listening intently.

"Yes," — "Yes," — "Yes,— " she half whispered at intervals.

Then she closed her eyes and bent down her head until her temples rested upon the base of her palms and her finger tips touched upon the top of her head. For a long time she sat motionless, and one not in the secret of her occupation might have thought her asleep. Not so Topeltzin, however. He waited patiently until at last she had raised her head again.

"Yes, I have the message," she said, again addressing the invisible person, "but of far greater moment is the fact that I have found you once more, that again our souls commune, that still —"

"Azra!" interrupted the harsh voice of Topeltzin.

The girl shuddered but did not turn.

"It was not your voice, O Zilpan," she said. "Hold me, dear! It seems that I am leaving you."

"Azra!" again commanded Topeltzin.

This time she pressed her finger tips upon her eyes and sank back in her chair. When she took her fingers away she turned to him with a sigh and raised her eyes wearily to him.

"My lord, I salute you," she said and humbly and instantly arose, bowing her head before him with pathetic humility that a mother might use to a jailer who had her child in his power.

"You got a message just now," charged Topeltzin.

"Yes, my lord. To-day there came over the eastern bridge into the Pearl City a tall dark stranger."

"Black Eagle," supplemented the high priest.

"That is it. I could not see the name clearly in Zilpan's mind except that it was a great black bird. I do not know eagles very well, my lord, nor does Zilpan, I think. With him were Father Zolcoma and soldiers and that other gray-haired stranger of whom I have told you."

"Professor Raymon," said Topeltzin. "What other news?"

"Zilpan has just learned that there is an underground passage from the plateau above the Red City to the white canyon. Through this passage Black Eagle came, and through it Father Zolcoma plans in some way to rescue Prince Izon. Just how, either Zilpan has not yet discovered, or if he did try to tell me I did not read it plainly."

"It seems to me," said Topeltzin dryly, "that you spend more of your time exchanging personal messages with Zilpan than in the service of our gods."

"Ah, they are hard gods, with hearts of stone!" cried the girl, "and they who would serve them must know sorrow and tears without end! Is not Tezcatlipoca yet satisfied? Listen, my lord. I have been patient. Zilpan has been patient. How soon may we have our reward? It has been two years now, since, upon our wedding morn and before we had even opportunity to know the clasp of each other's arms, the statue of Tezcatlipoca, before which you wedded us, spoke and commanded us to be driven apart, commanded Zilpan to secret service in the Pearl City, and me to this dreary prison. Since that day I have never seen his face except with my soul across all those weary miles that intervene, and you promised us if we did Tezcatlipoca's service loyally and well, that the time of Zilpan's exile should be short and that we should soon again be united."

"Two years is not so long a service," replied Topeltzin. "Think you that Tezcatlipoca will admire your ungrateful spirit? Since childhood, both you and Zilpan were raised in luxury and ease, and were taught by me the cultivation of the mind faculty which enables you now to be in communion with your Zilpan daily. You have nothing else to do, in fact, but talk with him."

"Yes, my lord," she replied piteously, "to talk with him and to long for him, to mourn and grieve for the sight of his dear eyes, the touch of his dear hand. Ah, my lord, you taught us these things, it is true, and you brought us together that we might learn to love, and when we had learned to love — which was your purpose — when we had learned that life for both depended upon the love of the other, then you tore us apart, knowing that through this gift that you bred in us we must be together in thought, always, and so become a mere carrier of news for you. Oh, it is cruel, cruel! Have mercy!"

She sank upon her knees. Topeltzin had a sharp reproof upon his tongue, but before he could utter it she sprang suddenly to her feet again.

"Yes, my beloved, I hear you!" she cried, rushing to the window.

She seemed to listen intently for a moment, then, turned to him in an agony of fear.

"Oh, he is in danger!" she cried. "He is calling to me, he is telling me that his hiding place is discovered, that they have burst in upon him and are taking him away. He is fighting them! I can see no more! I cannot find his mind! O-o-o-o-h!" and with a shriek she fell forward, fainting, upon the table.

Topeltzin paid no attention to her, except to summon

her maid, then hastening to his own room, he ordered Helox, that captain of the guards who had befriended the Christian captives, before him.

"Captain," he commanded, "there is a subterranean passage leading from the upper plateau to Luxtol. You will at once detail a company of your soldiers to deploy over the surface of the plateau, and to stay there until the opening to this passage is found. You will go with them yourself to insure that the work is done faithfully. There will be a promotion for the man who finds the entrance. I will give you three days. In addition to the hunting for this entrance, you will put a guard upon the cliff by night and by day. It is probable that Black Eagle will come that way, and his appearance may reveal the entrance to the underground passage; at any rate, he must not be able to get over the top of the cliff without discovery. If he returns he must not be molested, but allowed to go to his own apartments without interference. Go, and the reward or vengeance of the gods will be yours even as you succeed or fail."

Captain Helox saluted and withdrew.

It was nearing midnight when Black Eagle drew himself up under the two overlapping rocks which concealed the entrance to the crevasse. He was astonished to see a row of flaming torch-lights, not over twenty feet apart, all along the walls of the cliff, and bobbing lights scattered here and there over the rugged surface of the plateau. While he stood pondering these things, and before he emerged from the black shadow which concealed him, he heard a low, cautious voice at his side. Turning quickly, he recognized in the half-light the countenance of Captain Helox.

"Be cautious, brother," said the captain. "Keep in the cover of this rock when you get out, and work your way among the shadows to a point as far distant from this as possible before you reveal yourself. Do not disclose the location of this opening. I am the only man in the Red City who knows it, and three days from now I lose my captainship because it will not be found. But do not fear. You are not to be harmed in any way, not even questioned, for the present, at least. The first soldier to whom you apply will supply you with his scaling ladder, although you must not intimate that you know this. Wait a minute until I move around to the other side where I can conceal you as you emerge and crawl behind the rock. Good-bye and God be with you!"

CHAPTER XIII
ON THE PARAPET

BLACK Eagle on his return to the palace joined Izon immediately, and told him the good news about Professor Raymon and sent a note in English to the overjoyed Mariam and Isabel.

The cousins went to the gardens, waiting with eager curiosity for Black Eagle to join them. They were seated near one of the fountains where they could see the archway from which he usually emerged, when Mariam rose to her feet with an exclamation of pleasure.

"They are coming at last," she said as Izon appeared. She always saw Izon first in any group.

The man with him was not Black Eagle, who was detained by a sprained ankle, but Topeltzin. It was the first time that the high priest had seen fit to join the girls in an informal way, and they found him to be a man of remarkable social gifts, entertaining and brilliant, but with strange, compelling eyes which held them in a fascination which they realized but could not resist; eyes that attracted while they repelled, and warned while they conquered.

He began his talk with an apology for the manner in which they had been received on the day of their entry into the Red City, and Izon smiled as the high priest glibly explained that their beloved prince, while on a hunting expedition, had been attacked by enemies and rescued by his faithful subjects. The girls and Black Eagle had been captured with these enemies and their execution had been ordered for this, and according to an ancient law, as a part of the celebration in which the prince's loving subjects expressed their joy at his rescue by hailing him as a god. Izon had it upon his lips to riddle Topeltzin's clever explanation with sarcasm, but it was no part of his plan to make the girls acquainted with his danger and besides, he was overflowing with the details of the good news which he could not tell the girls in the high priest's company. He soon found an opportunity to separate himself and Mariam from the others and as Topeltzin watched them turn into one of the leafy bypaths, he frowned as did Zaliza, who was jealously watching them from a balcony. Mariam's hand rested on Izon's arm, and his head was bent towards her, the two making as pretty a picture as one might wish to view. Isabel glowed with pride in them.

"How I love to see those two together!" she exclaimed to Topeltzin.

His countenance instantly cleared as she looked up at him.

"They are indeed a handsome couple," he assented. "Your cousin is an exceptionally beautiful girl. I suppose she has had no lack of lovers, as your deities and ours seem to ordain these matters alike," he added with apparent carelessness.

"Nothing serious, I believe," Isabel laughingly replied, not suspecting the sinister personal interest that lay back of the question. "Really, she seems to be more interested in the prince than in any one with whom I have seen her."

"So I should judge," said Topeltzin dryly. "It seems to have been a very quickly ripened friendship."

"It could scarcely be otherwise, under the circumstances," replied Isabel, and she explained how they had met, told him of the loss of Mariam's father, and then the conversation led naturally to the subject of Professor Raymon's theories in regard to the Aztecs, and his life-long search, culminating in this trip.

Topeltzin's eyes sparkled with appreciation.

"Your uncle must have been a wonderfully gifted man," he said. "I should like to have met him. It would have been a pleasure to tell him that every one of his theories was correct to the last detail, even to his deduction that the son of Montezuma escaped with us, aided by our gods, although he scarcely deserved this as he had deserted them to worship the far-away and invisible deities of the Christians. He was right even to his surmise that when our forefathers were driven out of Mexico they carried with them the greater amount of their treasure, which the greedy Spaniards supposed they had captured."

"That is the one thing which has puzzled me," replied Isabel. "You came away with abundant riches, and you found here deposits of gold which I am told have not their equal in all the world. Why, then, with so much wealth at your command, do you not utilize this great power in a larger way? Why do you remain

ON THE PARAPET

hidden here when with this unlimited treasure you could command everything the outer world could offer?"

Topeltzin smiled.

"The outer world," he replied, "has nothing that we want. On the other hand we have the one thing for which they will kill and burn and devastate. This is the fruit of the teachings of your wonderful God, and the experience of our ancestors with Cortez and his followers taught us a bitter lesson in that branch of education. Had the Aztecs of Mexico not been rich, they would still burn the sacred fire upon the heights of Anahuac. In view of this, we have learned not to invite disaster, especially with no chance of gain. Name any luxury which your world possesses and I can show you the utmost refinement of it here, besides many other means of enjoyment not dreamed of by your people. We have here an ideal existence and there are two classes, the rulers and the ruled. The masters *live* in the fullest sense of that word, but we are wise enough to give the slaves so much pleasure that they are content. It matters not what the form of government, these two classes always exist. Here we are blunt; we call the lower class slaves; in your country they are called by another name but they exist just the same. Are they as happy as ours?"

The argument was unanswerable, to Isabel, at least. She was bound to acknowledge the force of his reasons against communion with the outer world.

"But," she persisted, "do you not lack one great luxury after all? Is not travel and change of scene essential for the highest enjoyment of life?"

"Partly so," he answered, "but we have them here, though in different forms. As for change of scene, we are about to have one presently which may convince you of the variety we enjoy. Our gods enjoy diversion; look! you may see them at play!"

While talking they had approached the parapet overlooking the river. Across from them arose the mighty cliffs of the canyon, seeming to reach the very skies, and as Isabel's gaze swept up the stupendous chasm, that same thrill of awe and wonder passed over her which she invariably felt when viewing this sublime spectacle from any new angle.

"Do you see nothing unusual?" inquired Topeltzin.

ON THE PARAPET

"Nothing, except that perhaps the coloring of the cliffs seems slightly different to-day."

"Look again, carefully up the canyon as far as you can see. Do you note that small cloud which is approaching?"

She looked, and smiled, turning to him with the eager curiosity of a child whose interest has been aroused.

"I do see it now," she replied with pleased anticipation, "but what does it signify?"

The question was scarcely uttered when the answer came, but not from Topeltzin. With startling swiftness the cloud increased in volume until it filled the entire upper canyon, and a sharp blast of wind in Isabel's face warned her that it would soon reach them. The rapidity of the change from bright sunlight and balmy air was almost incredible. Lightnings were darting now in every direction in the body of the rolling cloud, and with the same flashing speed a shrieking tornado enveloped them. Isabel started in terror to fly to the shelter of the palace, but inky darkness fell upon them and the sweep of the wind hurled her against the parapet, where she crouched, closing her eyes to the vivid flashes of lightning and her ears to the crashing thunder. Terrific as had been some of the storms which swept through the Mexican valley, awe-inspiring as had been many of the convulsions of nature which Mariam and Isabel had witnessed, they gave her no idea of this raging tempest. It would have been impossible for her to have formed a conception of the concentrated fury of these canyon cloud throes. Confined between the walls of the gorge, the forces, as though in wrath at being unable to expand in every direction, hurled themselves with Titanic anger upon everything in their path. They came with the swiftness of thought and they tore and rended as if with the ruthless hand of an infuriated and all-powerful demon. Isabel, always emotional, screamed in terror, but she felt that her voice was lost in the tumult which raged about them. Suddenly, however, there came a lull, and through it Topeltzin's deep voice.

"You are not to be afraid, Isabel," he called, "of man or nature or the gods while I am with you. Behold my power."

ON THE PARAPET

She looked up amazed. Topeltzin had sprung upon the parapet, and now stood with outstretched arms, as though commanding the very elements. His rich costume was ablaze with a greenish lurid light which illuminated the scene and made his form, with its towering head-dress, seem colossal. Flames wrapped him, wavering and leaping from every point of his robe, and giving to him a majesty that awed the trembling onlooker. He raised his arms and thundered:

"Back from us, ye wild winds and thunder bolts! I command you by the power of Tezcatlipoca!"

An apparent miracle followed upon the words. The fearful storm raged around them in a vast circle, but in the space they occupied all was calm. They seemed to to be the centre of the vortex which this magician had made in the hurricane. Isabel straightened up, her eyes dilated and her lips parted, her heart beating violently and her breath panting, thrilled and raised to an emotional frenzy by excitement.

"It is marvellous," she cried hysterically. "What mighty power, that even the elements obey!"

"Power!" cried Topeltzin. "You have not yet

seen power, child! I will suspend all the laws of nature. Behold the might of our gods! Look! Can the rulers of your outer world accomplish this?"

He turned to an adjacent watch tower with a shout to command attention and issued a crisp order in Aztec. A bright flame blazed upon the summit of the tower. A glowing mass presently came falling toward them which, as it rolled over, seemed to be a white-hot boulder as large as a man's head. Topeltzin leaping lightly down to it, reached forth and to Isabel's horror grasped the fiery boulder and held it out upon his hand without the slightest sign of pain. He poised it with smiling ease, while she could plainly see the intense heat that radiated from the glowing mass. Awe and terror struggled for the mastery over her. Topeltzin seemed on fire from head to foot, while he still held the glowing ball, and the girl's knees trembled as she felt that she was in the presence of some superhuman power. The boulder was suddenly tossed into the basin of a fountain, and as it struck the water it burst with a loud report, while a cloud of hissing steam rolled up, evidence of the intense heat.

"Power!" Topeltzin exclaimed again. "Look!"

On the Parapet—Topeltzin's Magic

ON THE PARAPET

He sprang upon the parapet, and drawing his sword, reached its point far out to a projecting ledge. He leaned over the precipice upon the sword. The long Spanish blade, evidently a relic of the Conquest, bent under his weight, and it seemed a fearfully perilous risk he took in depending upon its frail support.

"Now, Isabel," he commanded, "gaze steadily upon me. Behold my power as high priest of mighty Tezcatlipoca!"

He was leaning out almost at right angles. He was supported only by his right arm, holding the sword against the ledge. The jagged rocks of the precipice, and the river hundreds of feet below, meant a terrible death if he should fall. He seemed to mutter some incantation, and then let the point of the sword drop and remained suspended in the air. Isabel shrieked. Her strength deserted her and she slowly sank to her knees, gazing at Topeltzin where he lay upon air against the background of the rushing storm. An interminable moment this apparition lasted, and then slowly, evenly, the high priest arose to an upright position, his garments still flaming, and with folded arms stood triumphant before her. His eyes glittered with the baleful glare of some noxious serpent. Isabel felt herself held with such fascination as draws the fluttering bird into the reach of poisoned fangs. Topeltzin smiled, and his smile itself, with the gleaming teeth behind it, seemed but a part of the dread spell he had riveted upon her.

The hand of Providence reached out to save Isabel. An awful change suddenly came over Topeltzin's countenance. His eyes seemed to start from their sockets, the smile upon his lips became a hideous grin, and his features worked convulsively, his aspect becoming all at once that of some lost spirit cowering before a hated superior power. His left hand clutched at his heart. He reached out his right hand, pointing upwards, and Isabel's eyes followed the direction. The greatest wonder of all that she had seen followed to her rapt vision. High up in air, directly over the scene and seeming to float in the black clouds that encompassed them, a golden object, colossal, glowing, gathering to itself domination over all the mystery that had preceded it, shone through and yet against the black background.

"The accursed cross!" shrieked Topeltzin, shaking his clenched hand at the vision.

His livid face became still more ghastly and he tot-

ON THE PARAPET

tered forward, falling with a crash from the parapet to the spot where Isabel knelt. There he lay, writhing like some wounded animal in a death agony. Isabel, overwhelmed with thankfulness for this vision that had broken the spell, raised her hands to the bright image. But it did not remain. Its mission over, it faded away, and the appalling blackness once more settled around her with its snapping of livid lightning and its tumult of deafening thunder. Her tortured mind could stand no more and she sank, fainting, across the body of the high priest.

CHAPTER XIV
IN THE LABYRINTH

WITHOUT paying much attention to where they were going, Izon and Mariam had wandered into the labyrinth, a winding path that, at first apparently open, became gradually closer hedged on each side by thickly set, impenetrable shrubbery. The path wound upon itself like the convolutions of a shell, with innumerable cunningly laid out bypaths that led only to blind pockets, so that even those who were familiar with the place sometimes wandered for an hour in its recesses before they could find their way out.

When the storm broke upon the palace grounds in its sudden fury, the prince cast about him for one of the grottos, but quickly recognized that he and Mariam were in the labyrinth. He turned to escape from its maze but took the wrong direction and the path he had chosen ended in an angle of the cliff. The blackness of the storm settled upon them, and inasmuch as the cliff gave them some shelter from the wind it was folly to attempt to proceed any farther for the time being. Mariam was thinly clad, but trailing at his back her companion had a voluminous cloak that, though a heavy impediment, was lightly worn because it was a part of the insignia of his high station. For once in his life he thanked the vagaries of courtly fashion for this accoutrement. Mariam, cowering before the incessant lightnings and the thunder, and shivering from the blasts that tore at them, found this cloak drawn strongly around her in the clasp of Izon's arm, and herself pressed closely to him in the angle of the rock. Instantly she nestled closer to that protection in her terror, and then, suddenly realizing what she had done, shocked and amazed at herself, she struggled to be free, only to find that firm clasp unrelenting. "My love," whispered the gentle voice of Izon, "do not deny me this sweet privilege — the right to guard and protect you now and always."

For an instant Mariam was overwhelmed, not alone by what he had said, but by the flood of thrilling self-consciousness that came upon her; for all at once she knew that she had loved him from the moment that she had met him. It was very simple, now that he had

PRINCE IZON opened her eyes to what she had known but had not realized. Why, how natural it had seemed, there at first, to yield to that embrace, and how natural it seemed now! Izon recognized with trembling ecstasy, the sweet meaning of this new relaxation and, lifting the cloak that he had drawn above her head, he bent down to her and pressed a kiss upon her forehead. Lower still he bent, and simply, trustingly, Mariam raised her lips to his. Thus was their compact sealed. They had no need for words, but, clasped in the ecstatic embrace of pure love, awaiting the passing of the storm, nor thinking its duration too long, Mariam could feel his heart beating against her bosom and knew, without the formal message of lame speech, that its every beat was true and for love of her.

It was not until the storm had lashed out its rage, and that darkness had begun to be displaced by that lurid yellow atmosphere which, with its uncanny glow, follows electrical disturbances, that they spoke.

"See," said Izon, pointing to where, in the upper canyon, the clearer light was beginning to show through, "it is a sign that, though our skies be dark, there is a light to come. It cannot be that, after Providence has guided us to each other by such strange means, we are not to live happily together. Dangers threaten us, but I believe in the power of our God against these idol-worshippers."

"Who could doubt Him now?" replied Mariam, "since my father has been miraculously preserved and He has sent you to me?"

They were turning now to retrace their steps, and Mariam in placing her arm upon Izon's shoulder found it wet.

"This will not do," she said with anxiety. "While you were keeping the rain from me, it was reaching you. We must go in at once."

So saying she gayly led him down the path. They were like two happy children in this new-found world of theirs. All difficulties that might beset them dwindled to nothingness in the face of this great joy that had come to them. The storms of life were but fleeting things, that must give way before the eternal sunshine of the love which they knew must ever be shining on the other side of all clouds. The glow that succeeded the evening storm, to lighten the world for a space before the dusk of the evening, enabled them to

PRINCE IZON

pick their way from the labyrinth, and they hastened to the palace. Izon would have prolonged his adieus, but Mariam, concerned about his recent exposure, drove him away in a pretty tyranny and hastened to her own apartments in that rapturous exultation which comes but once in a lifetime.

The prince was about to descend the stairway when he saw in the dim light a bulky figure staggering toward him. He advanced hastily and found that it was Topeltzin, bearing the still unconscious Isabel in his arms.

"What is the matter?" asked Izon with quick anxiety.

"It was an electrical shock," explained the high priest haltingly, then muttered, "The gods deserted me."

He was but barely recovered, and the exertion of carrying Isabel was at the moment almost sufficient to overtax him. Nevertheless, it was with some reluctance that he relinquished his burden to the prince, and disappeared.

The shifting of Isabel from Topeltzin's arms to those of Izon revived her slightly, and at the doorway through which Mariam had just passed, she struggled down,

IN THE LABYRINTH

not knowing where she was, but imbued with an unconscious idea of resistance. The moment her feet touched the tiles, she found her great weakness, but, her eyes opening, she turned them up to her companion, and finding that it was the prince, whom she had come to regard as a dear and trusted brother, her gratitude at her deliverance overwhelmed her. Because of her helplessness she cast her arms about his neck, and Izon supported her with mingled pity and apprehension lest the shock might have had some serious effect upon her.

It was all natural enough, but to Black Eagle, whose mainsprings of emotion were still dominated by the influence of his savage ancestry, the sight was one that seared. It was at this unfortunate moment that he mounted the stairway. He stood rooted to the spot, his jealousy suddenly flaming up and mastering his judgment. All that he knew of Izon, all that he knew of Isabel, facts that should have made him understand or at least await an understanding, were swept away in the sudden hurricane of his passion. He controlled himself with difficulty, but, after all, his hurt was more than his rage. His finger nails sunk deeply into his palms, then silently, but torn and rent within by the whirlwind of emotions as violent as the storms which had just passed, he turned away.

Izon, all unconscious of this, beat a hasty summons at Isabel's door, and after a brief explanation to her maids, went to his own apartments. He met Black Eagle in the corridor. The chieftain passed him by without a word. Izon noted the glare that was given him but attached no meaning to it, thinking that perhaps his friend might be preoccupied with plans for their escape. The process of thought and the planning always made him taciturn. In the meantime Isabel, carefully tended and put to bed, with Mariam sitting anxiously by her side, passed into a delirium that lasted until the following morning. The shock of all that she had seen and endured had been too much for her. She was not well enough versed in the natural sciences to conceive or even to question how Topeltzin's apparent miracles had been wrought, and she could not but accept him as he represented himself to be, a creature of awesome power, almost a god, and indeed rising superior to the natural laws of the Deity himself. He had not only shaken her faith but had inspired in her a terror of himself, and the thought

IN THE LABYRINTH

that by his mighty power he could compel her instant obedience, could bend her will to himself like wax, was in itself enough, for the time being, to dethrone her tottering reason.

Had she but known, each of the mysteries with which he had overawed her was suscetpible of natural explanation. But Isabel, brought up simply, could not know this, and it is small wonder that she emerged from the delirium with the terrifying belief that Topeltzin was all-powerful, a belief made all the more terrifying in that she knew his to be an evil power. When she regained consciousness she tried to persuade herself that the whole thing had been a hideous dream brought on by the terrors of the storm, but her recollection of it was too vivid. Then, too, Mariam told her how Izon had taken her from the arms of the high priest. Her first impulse upon this was to tell Mariam all that had happened, but at the moment she felt too weak to enter upon such an exciting subject, and mature thought encouraged her to silence. It would do no good at present and it would only distress Mariam. She would wait — and watch.

CHAPTER XV
THE HAIL DANCE

CAPTAIN HELOX, busily engaged in the inspection of the new palace guard detail, which had just come on duty, paused and smiled genially as he saluted a gay procession headed by Zaliza and a group of young nobles emerging from the palace gates. It was a brilliant throng that swept by the captain on its way into the city. Izon, resplendent in his princely costume, had declined the gold-decked litter which usually bore him, and was walking, surrounded by court beauties in the midst of whom Mariam and Isabel shone resplendent. Black Eagle, stately and tall, unbent from his usual dignity, and, suppressing his jealousy, joined the mirth and persiflage that passed from one to another of the merry band as it crossed the plaza on the way to the shops and markets of the Red City. "Youth and beauty," quoth the doughty captain to himself as he watched them, "youth and beauty go together, only," he muttered with a stifled sigh, "what will the ending

THE HAIL DANCE

be for some of them? — will Tezcatlipoca, aided by such temptations, win or lose?" With a thoughtful brow he resumed his official duties.

There were two large plazas in the Red City, one, upon which fronted the high priest's palace, being the same into which Izon had made his triumphal entry, while the second was about a mile up the canyon. A broad paved street flanked on one side by a parapet overlooking the river, and on the other by the canyon walls, connected these plazas, and the marts of the Red City occupied the wall side, through its entire length.

It was the middle of the forenoon; both streets and shops were filled with the teeming life of the Red City. As the party from the palace traversed the first plaza and entered the shops, the vast throng stood aside, with respectful obeisances to Izon. Many were the glances of admiration cast upon the Spanish beauties, while Zaliza and her girl friends evoked an almost equal share. The young Aztec nobles surrounding their fair friends were picked youths of Ixtol, distinguished alike by birth and grace of manners. Detailed by Topeltzin to aid in entertaining the prince, they soon found their occupation one of entrancing interest in vying with each other, and with Izon and Black Eagle, for the smiles of their fair companions. These being true daughters of Eve, and selected also from the nobility, to assist in the entertainment, all of them distributed their smiles fairly on the eager youths. As has often happened on like occasions, the rank alone of Izon would not have won him more than the rest, had not he outshone them by his comeliness and wit.

Youth and beauty certainly reigned that morn in the Red City. The warm sunlight, tinted with the canyon colors, brilliantly illuminated the animated group as they entered shop after shop, pricing and buying whatever took their fancy. Here they found a vase, as tall as Black Eagle, around which he could not reach even his long arms; there plaques of gold set with mosaic or chased and fretted more skilfully than lies in the power of any European artist. They bought, too, bundles of quetzal feathers set in gold filigree, worn aigrette style, which were permitted only to the nobility; robes of delicate cotton fabric woven with small bird feathers in bright colors, lighter and downier than silk; household utensils of all kinds fashioned skilfully in gold; and pottery excelling anything Mariam or Isabel had ever seen in Mexico.

Entering the second plaza they found it crowded with people in holiday attire. The centre of attraction was a group of jugglers around which the crowd had gathered, the majority standing in the rear of a circle of seats reserved for those highest in rank. With gestures and cries of admiring homage to Izon, his party was conducted to these seats. They were soon being shown an exhibition of skill, dexterity, and strength that delighted the athletic Izon and Black Eagle, and drew admiring cheers from the others. Stimulated by the presence of the royal party, the jugglers, the most skilful in the world, showed themselves at their best. As a climax the leader announced that in honor of the representative of Tezcatlipoca and his party, they would exhibit their greatest and most difficult feat, the ascension into the air of one of their number.

A shout of delight greeted this announcement. This special performance was shown at long intervals only and usually in honor of some great dignitary. Only the elder among those present had seen it, but its fame had

PRINCE IZON

reached all except Black Eagle and the Spanish girls, who appealed to Zaliza for information.

"I have never seen it," she said, "but my father once told me it was very wonderful. He said that one of the men actually ascended into the air and then floated down, apparently supported only by a smoky vapor."

By this time the plaza had become densely crowded and every available window and housetop was occupied by spectators, desirous of witnessing the performance. All eyes were fixed upon the jugglers and tumblers, forty-seven in number. Two of them, the leader and the youth who was to make the ascension, were attired in flowing robes, covered with cabalistic emblems, that of the youth being also distinguished by its glittering golden scales. The others wore close-fitting suits. Suddenly at the signal, the entire band was thrown into apparent confusion. Leaping and shouting, they whirled about with such rapidity that the eyes of the observers were confused in following their gyrations, excepting Black Eagle, who was accustomed to similar scenes among his own people. Fifteen of the athletes suddenly stood in line shoulder to shoulder. At a signal each man

THE HAIL DANCE

swiftly passed his arms around the neck of his comrade on either side. Another signal, and the men at each end ran together, the line bending into a circle, the ends joining as they came together. Facing the centre, the fifteen made a compact circle. Instantly twelve of their comrades sprang upon their shoulders, locking their arms around each others' necks, all likewise facing to the centre. They were followed in bewildering rapidity by eight others, who surmounted the twelve, climbing with the agility of monkeys. The eight men were followed by six more, surmounting the eight, and finally by four more surmounting the six, all uttering the sharp cries peculiar to tumblers. They followed each other so closely that a huge living cone seemed to rise like magic out of the earth until it stood towering about twenty-five feet in height.

"How do those men at the base stand the weight?" asked Isabel of Black Eagle. "I should think they would be crushed."

"Oh, no," he answered, "there are fifteen of them and thirty above. Thus each man sustains the weight of only two, which is a trifle to these athletes."

The shouts of admiration which had greeted the

completion of the human pyramid ceased and a tense silence ensued. The two leaders had disappeared.

"Look!" suddenly cried Zaliza, pointing to the apex. As thousands followed her gaze, a light-colored dense smoke issued from the hollow human cone. It ascended, spreading out, but as a light wind partially blew it aside, the youth with the glittering robe was seen standing above the topmost four men, the vapor below him being his only apparent support. The amazed spectators had scarcely time to realize this before these four suddenly released their holds and, facing about, boldly leaped to the ground. They were followed in turn by the six below them, and so on until the cone had melted away. As the athletes jumped down in turn, the youth followed them, apparently floating down in the smoke until he finally rested on the shoulders of the leader, who was now discovered in the centre of the fifteen. For a minute the youth stood bowing his acknowledgments of the storm of admiring cheers from the throng. Then he too leaped down and the entire band left the plaza.

None were more hearty in their applause than Izon

THE HAIL DANCE

and his party. Black Eagle alone was so prefunctory in doing his share that Isabel asked him,

"Don't you think it wonderful?"

"Yes," he replied smiling. "It was a wonderful exhibit of skill and strength, but if you refer to the apparent standing in the air, there was nothing wonderful about that."

"How so? Explain!" came from many.

"My own people have used smoke for centuries to aid them in performing their festival feats," he said. "While they do not exhibit this one in particular, they perform another even more apparently wonderful. While dancing on the edge of a precipice of the canyon, perhaps a mile deep, they seem to step off the edge of the chasm, dance in the air, and return to the cliff."

"Now, Black Eagle," said Isabel with a mocking smile, "we will take your word for that, but will you kindly explain what it has to do with this thing we have just seen with our own eyes, the young man floating in the air right out there above us?"

"Of course," answered the chieftain quietly. "I do not know exactly what substance the leader burned to produce the peculiar smoke we saw, but I am confident that when the first circle was formed he and the youth were crouching in its centre and as the cone was forming the young man was climbing a pole as fast as his comrades went up."

A great shouting suddenly interrupted Black Eagle. A procession crossed the plaza headed by an officer of large stature, in brilliant accoutrements and followed by a number of Aztec nobles and by soldiers guarding a prisoner. As the captive and his escort passed near Izon, the prince started, and crying "Tezco! — my dear friend — alive!" rushed toward him, thrust the guards aside, and embraced him with the deepest affection.

Gautemotzin, the officer in the lead, was by birth the rightful ruler of the Red City. Yielding to his baser nature, he had but feebly opposed Topeltzin's rise to supreme power. As evidence of the high priest's diplomacy, however, he had made the descendant of Montezuma's famous nephew the prefect of the Red City outside the palace domain. One strong tie bound the two, the necessity for furnishing entertainments as

THE HAIL DANCE

frequently as possible to the masses of the people. Confined as they were, such diversions were absolutely necessary to the maintenance of the autocratic power wielded by the high priest and his lieutenant. For the first time in a long period, both the rulers now had ample material for their purpose. The capture of Izon, and the great festivals accompanying his entrance, his stay, and his ending, aroused the keenest anticipations, all looking forward to saturnalias still greater, while Gautemotzin now had the means at his command to satisfy their immediate craving for cruel pleasures.

In the massacre of Izon's band in the lower canyon, one other had survived besides the prince, Black Eagle, and the girls. A young noble named Tezcotzin, in defending the prince had received a spear thrust in the shoulder and lay insensible among the dead, when Gautemotzin, who led the raiders, found him living, and brought him to the Red City.

Violent was the dispute between the high priest and Gautemotzin regarding the disposal of the captive. Topeltzin at first wished to hold him as a substitute for Izon in case the latter repudiated his religion, but, noting the scar from his wound, which unfitted him for sacrifice, he yielded Tezcotzin to the tender mercies of the prefect.

The prisoner was carefully treated until he had fully recovered, his existence being concealed from Izon and his friends. Gautemotzin, with the keenest pleasure, now began his preparations to utilize the captive for his own gratification and that of the people. He had assembled the council, and when the captive was brought before it, had formally given him the option of life by repudiating his religion, or otherwise, death. As Tezcotzin in a ringing voice declared for death, the prefect could not refrain from an admiring look, as he announced that the captive would be given a chance for his life if he successfully passed the ordeal of the Hail Dance.

"The Hail Dance! The Hail Dance!" shouted the spectators, who had attended the council meeting, and they rushed out of the building, repeating the cry to the thousands in the plaza.

"The Hail Dance! What do they mean?" simultaneously asked the girls and Black Eagle, of Izon. The prince with a grave look replied that he knew

THE HAIL DANCE

only from distant hearsay that it was some apparently easy ordeal that a captive had the choice of undergoing or suffering death. If he succeeded in running the gantlet, he was allowed to return to the Pearl City, but many never passed through, for the pitfalls were numerous. As he ceased, the prince beckoned to the officer of his escort, and bade him lead his party, with the exception of Black Eagle, back to the palace, explaining to Mariam and Isabel that while there was no particular danger in their remaining, still the rougher elements in the city would participate in the coming affair, and they had better retire. Relieved by their safety, Izon and Black Eagle inquired regarding the identity of the victim, when they were interrupted by the shouts announcing the entry into the plaza of Gautemotzin, the council, and the captive himself.

Tezcotzin had no time to explain to Izon his survival of the massacre. Gautemotzin strode up, and while apparently showing the utmost deference to the prince, whispered, "My lord, do not attempt to use your power to interfere. All the soldiers I command could not prevent this mob now from tearing the prisoner to pieces, if deprived of their sport, and" — deepening his voice — "it might not be well for your friends."

Izon swiftly considered. He looked upon the thousands of faces, eager, some of them bestial, and keenly realized that Gautemotzin was right. Hundreds of the nobles who were mingled with the crowd knew his position, and while the masses considered him for the time being the god he was represented to be, they would not hesitate to rend to pieces the luckless Tezcotzin, the moment his protection was withdrawn.

"Tezco," he whispered, still embracing his friend, "be of good cheer; many have run the gantlet and I shall be at the end of the line to receive you. God be with you."

Black Eagle was standing near, ready to help, and curiously examining one of the boughs which attendants were distributing through the crowd. It was a branch from a native shrub, about three feet long, terminating in several twigs, each tipped with a small round seed pod. It looked harmless enough, but when at Black Eagle's request, Izon swished the pellets against the chieftain's face, it stung like swiftly driven hail.

THE HAIL DANCE

Extending beyond the second plaza, for over a mile up the canyon until it reached the ramparts of the Red City, was a wide shelf or ledge, that by years of labor had been made into a street. Flanked on one side by a parapet, it was lined on the other by rows of houses, the homes of the nobility. Terraced gardens extended up the canyon slope, and gay colored awnings of cotton cloth, shading doors and windows, added a charm to the beauty of the canyon tints. Below the parapet, the walls at first did not drop perpendicularly, but sloped down to a second ledge parallel to the street above. This ledge was only a few feet wide, and was used as a passage for the porters and other bearers of heavy burdens, from the gold dredges on the banks of the river. The haughty nobility would not tolerate these slaves on their promenade, so in course of time it had become a well worn trail averaging about five feet in width. It had no parapet, and from the outer edge of the cliff dropped sheer down hundreds of feet to the foaming torrent and jagged rocks below. This long trail was now lined on the wall side by thousands of the Red City men, each holding one of the hail boughs;

standing shoulder to shoulder, they reached from the plaza to the ramparts.

The parapet and street above were filled with the populace, excepting the priesthood and Topeltzin's court. The high priest, while cruel enough to enjoy any sport involving the suffering of others, was wily enough to forbid any of his entourage to participate, thus leaving all the glory to Gautemotzin. The older men, the women and children, thronged the upper street, and many, unable to get a place on the parapet, had climbed over it to rough and even dangerous perches on the steep slope that led to the trail below. All seemed animated with the holiday spirit. Laughter, singing, and shouting rent the air.

Izon entered the adjacent house of one of the nobles, by whom he was received with the usual deference. The prince, on stating that he desired to view the proceedings without being noticed, was furnished a long cloak and hood similar to those worn by the priests. Thus attired he walked down the upper street accompanied by Black Eagle. They passed in the rear of the crowd, but paused as they heard a group of young nobles discussing the coming ordeal.

THE HAIL DANCE

"By Tezcat," one of the young men cried, "I believe that fellow will win."

"A hundred quills that he does n't," cried another, and the wager was quickly taken by the first speaker.

"Gautemotzin told me," said a third youth, "that he himself would be the last man in the line, and you all know what that means — no Christian will ever get past him."

"A thousand quills that he will," said a fourth. "If ever I saw a good runner it is this same Tezcotzin. Such legs and chest this town can hardly boast."

"He is right," said Izon to his friend as they pursued their way. "Tezcotzin is descended from a family of famous runners. His ancestors in the days of Montezuma brought fresh fish from the gulf to the capital in one day with only three relays, and were finally ennobled. I feel confident that if treated fairly he will run the gantlet successfully, so let us go to the other end to see that he gets fair play from Gautemotzin."

Unnoticed they reached the vicinity of the gates. Looking over the parapet they noted that, in fact, Gautemotzin was the last man in the line and that he

PRINCE IZON stood opposite a particularly dangerous bend in the trail.

"See," whispered Izon, "the malignity of it — if Tezcotzin gets thus far, he will be exhausted and the slightest misstep will hurl him over."

Black Eagle did not reply. He was intently watching Gautemotzin. "Look!" he suddenly hissed, grasping the prince's arm, "he has tied a cord to a rock, which he has thrown over the cliff, where it hangs a few feet below. He has placed his foot upon the other end. The cord lies across the trail, invisible to any one approaching. As Tezcotzin runs up, the wretch can raise his end of the cord, and trip him over the bend."

A mighty shout from the crowd at the plaza end of the street greeted Tezcotzin, as he appeared for the ordeal. A loin cloth covered his hips and thighs, and the superb physique thus displayed appealed to the spectators only as the promise of good sport. It was quickly noted that a short javelin was fastened to his breast, the point touching under his chin, compelling him to hold his head erect, while his hands were attached to his waist by thongs that left them free to swing, but prevented him from raising them higher than his shoulders.

THE HAIL DANCE

It was thus apparent that no bending of the head or shielding with the hands would ward off the shower of hail-like pellets in his face. That no retreat or pause was possible was evidenced by the presence of two guards that were to follow him with spears levelled at his back.

For a moment a tense silence ensued, and then a pandemonium of sounds broke forth as Tezcotzin dashed down the pathway. Every man in the line held his bough aloft, and as the victim passed, brought it down diagonally against his face.

At first the sensation was like running in a violent hail storm. Instinctively he tried to lift his hands to ward off the stinging pellets. The thongs around his wrists held his hands a tantalizing distance away. Instinctively he tried to bend his head. The sharp point of the javelin pierced his chin. His eyelids were struck repeatedly. If he closed them an instant, he risked going over the precipice, risked plunging into space over the steep angles of the narrow trail. He tried closing one eye at a time, but every few moments both were struck at once, and he would stagger in the agonizing effort to see his way.

PRINCE IZON

Men have been driven to madness and death by the mere steady falling of single drops of water on the head, but this torment was here increased a thousand-fold. The constant stinging, never-ceasing blows of the hail gradually so inflamed the skin of his face that it seemed to be scorching as though held before a fire.

The blows on his eyeballs became so constant that he could only dimly see his way under lids that were almost closed. Intense and more intense the agony became, until with failing breath he paused, but only for a moment, as the sharp thrust of the spears in his back forced him onward.

No cry escaped him. His parched throat and failing breath prevented it, and even had he screamed, the sound would have been drowned by the howls of his tormentors, swelled by the shouts of the spectators on the parapet and those of the gamblers, who ran keeping pace with him, on the street above, changing the odds as he wavered, and then pushed forward.

He had now traversed about three-fourths of the course, but had lost all conception of the distance. Long-distance runners testify that they frequently have

THE HAIL DANCE

to look down to see if their legs are moving, to know they are still running.

Tezcotzin was only conscious of moving by the flame that seared his face, which he could mitigate only by pausing; but instantly to be thrust forward by the fierce goading of the spears in his back.

Suddenly, just as he felt his knees sinking, and another breath impossible, a stronger light than usual penetrated his almost closed eyes. His death-laden lids lifted, and for a second he saw the golden cross of the upper canyon, as it shone on this part of the trail. The sight nerves him for a final effort. It rallies the stamina inherited from fleet ancestors. He lunges forward, but is met by the most terrific onslaught of all. The biggest and strongest are here lined along the last part of the course. They are armed with the largest boughs. Fiercely, they bring them down until, gasping in agony, Tezcotzin sways from side to side. The burning hail strikes his face and eyes. His knees begin to bend and sink. The burning hail strikes his face and eyes. Gasping for breath through a foam-flecked mouth, he stumbles on. The burning hail — the burning hail! —

PRINCE IZON

Convulsed by agony, eyes now closed, hands feebly outstretched, goaded by the spears, he totters to the goal where Gautemotzin stands, and as his wavering feet strike the treacherous cord, he does not feel it, but only knows that he is falling forward, down, down with a consciousness of blissful rest.

As Gautemotzin raised from lifting the cord, he was seized in a powerful grasp. Twisting around he found himself in the clutch of Black Eagle. At the same moment Izon received the fainting form of Tezcotzin.

"Now, Gautemotzin," cried the prince, casting aside his cowl, "it is my turn to advise — Tezcotzin has won. I command you to open the gates and restore him to his waiting friends." Whispering, he added, "Obey, or I will proclaim your treachery to the entire city. You need not fear for me," he quickly added, "I pledge you my honor that I will return to the palace."

With a deep obeisance, the humbled Gautemotzin obeyed. Amid aloud acclaim, Tezcotzin was carried to the gates, and after a parting embrace and message from Izon, was delivered to his friends — guards of the

THE HAIL DANCE

Pearl City gates opposite those of the Red City. Prince Izon then, escorted by thousands of cheering people, returned with Black Eagle to the palace of the high priest.

CHAPTER XVI
BY MOONLIGHT

THE glory of the moonlight was upon all things in the canyon, filling it with mild radiance, borrowing from the warmly colored cliffs a rosy, trembling glow, changing into new and more beautiful tints as the queen of night swept higher in her royal progress, her silvery splendor flooding palaces and bridges and parapeted highways, and lingering with its greatest charm upon the vast, terraced gardens, where soft shadows vied with the fairy-lighted open spaces in mystic attractiveness. Isabel had stolen out to the terrace alone to ponder over the change which she had noticed for days in Black Eagle. From the stately and dignified, but ever cheerful, chieftain he had become morose and solitary, holding aloof from all his companions and especially from her, though when by chance he met her he was always exceedingly deferential. This changed demeanor and his evident suffering had aroused in her a pity which was none the less poignant because she could not fathom the cause of his altered attitude. She knew that whatever that cause might be it referred to her in some way, and, with the intuition which deceives no woman, she felt that the time must shortly come when there would be an explanation and when she must in some manner answer the question that he was sure to ask her.

While smiling at her certainty of what that answer must be, footsteps broke the current of her thoughts, and from one of the innumerable leafy paths the massive figure of Black Eagle appeared. When he saw Isabel he stopped for a moment, but retreat was barred by his pride and he came quickly on, resolved to pass her with a nod. She forestalled him in this by greeting him with the warmth that she assumed to be due to a friend of his standing.

"I'm so glad you came," she said cordially, "I have been growing quite lonely during the past half-hour."

Black Eagle was not one who could long dissemble where his emotions were concerned.

"I think you are mistaken," he bluntly replied. "I am not Prinze Izon. I just saw him wandering about the grounds as though seeking some one."

The scene that he had witnessed had rankled in him

until, when alone, he could think of nothing else. Under other circumstances he must have known that Izon was searching for Mariam. Isabel, whose back was turned to the moonlight which rested upon the face of Black Eagle, revealing there the play of his emotion, could not resist the mischievous impulse which so often swayed her. The serious regard she had given to the problem of Black Eagle's strange distress was swept away in an instant, and the desire to torment him came uppermost.

"I have not seen him — yet," she said indifferently.

"Yet!" he echoed bitterly. It was too much to be borne. He turned away from her abruptly, all the savage within him aroused to fury. "I will kill one of them," he muttered to himself.

Isabel, laughing, caught his arm. "Stay!" she invited him softly.

He turned to her with a half-articulate cry.

"Isabel!" he exclaimed. "I do not know why you are trying to torture me, but I cannot escape the knowledge that you are doing it, deliberately. You know and you cannot deny that you know, that I love you, have loved you from that first moment I met you upon the plains above. Through all the dangers that have beset

BY MOONLIGHT

us since, I have thought of you and of no one but you, by day and by night, in your presence and away, in all moods and times and places, until earth and sky are full of you, you, and nothing but you! 'Earth and sky,' Isabel! Do you know how much that means to one with the blood of a hundred chiefs in his veins? Do you know that it means my home, and the home that has sheltered my ancestors? What a glorious home! Floored by the wide level plain, roofed by the dome of the sky; their proud spirits disdaining to be bounded by less! Free, they were free! Free to stay or to fly where fancy dictates, or the wild chase leads, over the billowing plains on emerald sward, astride bounding steeds of fire that answered fire! Ah! that is life!"

His eyes were flashing and his breast heaving, and Isabel, following his every word in fascination, found her own trace of Indian blood bounding in eager sympathy. Her own eyes were dilated, and her own breath exhaling deeper and sharper. "It is so that I love you, Isabel," he continued, "I love you with all that wild sweeping fervor, that breadth and largeness that knows no boundaries save the stars above, and you are mine!" His voice no longer pleaded, it commanded. "Mine, and though Izon held you in his embrace, though death itself claimed you, I would seize you so, and make you mine!"

He ceased, and without knowing why or when, these two wild spirits found themselves clasped in a fervid embrace, burning lips upon burning lips, eyes flashing unto each the electric spark of love!

They seated themselves upon a bench nearby, and gradually drifted back, after their first transports were over, to the main idea which possessed them all, the fate that hung over Izon and possibly themselves, though Black Eagle found it difficult to remain upon the subject. Once or twice it occurred to him to question Isabel about the incident of the storm, although he had heard the details of the strange accident that had befallen her. Even this explanation had not driven away the stubborn idea that had then possessed his mind, but in the events of this evening he understood it perfectly, as, in fact, he would have understood in the beginning had he allowed himself to think.

However, while Isabel was planning aloud some way for them to escape surveillance when the time came for them to escape through the grotto, a mention of the

BY MOONLIGHT

prince reminded her of a forgotten errand, and she hurried away, promising to return in a few moments, leaving Black Eagle overwhelmed in the emotions of his own unfathomable delight.

He was not the only one who had Isabel in mind at that hour. Earlier in the evening Zeno had come to Topeltzin very mysteriously.

"I have come to ask your aid, my lord," he said, after the usual salutation.

Topeltzin, who was deep in calculations of his own, looked out at him from under shaggy brows.

"What have you learned about that underground passage from the White City to the grotto?" he demanded, ignoring Zeno's request.

"The soldiers are still searching for it, my lord."

"Three days! By Tezcat! Has Captain Helox been shorn of his rank, as I threatened him?"

"Not yet, my lord."

"Where is he?"

"In the soldiers' quarters, off duty at the present time, my lord."

"Take up his sword at once, and give him the uniform and accoutrements of a common soldier. I have certain suspicions of him, and I shall put him to a severe test. How long has he been off duty?"

"About six hours, my lord."

"Put him with the guard now on for the next twelve hours."

"Yes, my lord."

He shifted uneasily. Topeltzin, watching narrowly, smiled to himself.

"You began by requesting my aid. What is it?"

Zeno's relief made him brighten like a school-boy.

"My lord, you spoke some time ago about my using jealousy as a lever upon the Lady Zaliza, and recommended me to pay court to this Isabel."

"Yes."

"Well, you have set me a task of much difficulty and aggravation. I have made a few overtures to this dark-eyed Spanish rose, and have gotten myself well thorned for my pains. I scarcely know whether Isabel or Zaliza is the most vixenish, but I have a plan by which I am quite sure I can make a test, with your lordship's aid."

"Unfold your plan, my crafty Zeno."

"Well, it is this. To-night your lordship is to pre-

BY MOONLIGHT

side at a marriage celebration in the city, and although Zaliza has recently shown the utmost indifference to me, she has consented to meet me there. When the feast is about over, I will quietly leave and return to the palace, meeting Isabel by an ingenious plan which I have devised by the aid of Tequiepa, a young girl in the suite of our visitors, who stands in awe of priestly commands. If you will kindly tell Zaliza that you have something interesting to talk over with her, hinting that it concerns Izon, she will no doubt gladly return to the palace with you. At midnight, if you will so time it and will conduct her into the long central corridor and remain with her a few minutes in the shadows of her own doorway, I will pass with Isabel and give Zaliza an exhibition which may open her eyes somewhat."

Topeltzin was gravity itself, although he was amused as much as his evil nature permitted.

"What a plotting villain you are, my Zeno!" he bantered. "But you should be careful of this diplomatic tendency. It is a very dangerous thing. Some day you will do something brilliant and it will blind you. Have a care, Zeno; have a care! The gods may get jealous!"

Zeno reddened. He understood the jeer.

"But will you do me this favor, my lord?" he persisted.

Topeltzin was a man who knew no indecision. He could gain at least amusement in this adventure, and it might possibly further his own ends.

"I shall be present to applaud your comedy," he agreed. "I might tell you, however, that from what I gather you have handled this with all the delicacy of a man cracking a nut by toppling a cliff over it. If you have not already been able to arouse faint traces of jealousy in Zaliza, I judge you are about to make yourself ridiculous for nothing. You have evidently fallen into the clutches of Zite, our god of mischief!"

"Sir, if you think that I am precipitate — ?" faltered Zeno.

"No, proceed, my Zeno, I have no influence over Zite," laughed Topeltzin, and gave him the nod that meant dismissal.

CHAPTER XVII
ZENO'S LITTLE GAME

ISABEL found Mariam upon the balcony, reclining upon a feather-covered, swinging couch similar to a hammock, but far more comfortable. The moonlight that had turned canyon and gardens into a fairyland gently touched with its rosy glow her upturned face, spiritualizing its already exquisite beauty. There is an old superstition, firmly believed to this day by nearly every maiden of Mexico, that when sleeping in the moonlight the wraith of her own true love will appear and whisper his story to her, and of this tradition Isabel was instantly reminded. Slipping up to the hammock she laid her hand gently across the half drooping eyes that were gazing in pensive content out over the garden, and touched a kiss upon the curved lips. "Guess who," she said in playful gruffness. Mariam reached up and patted the hand with a laugh, and raised her arm about Isabel's neck as the latter bent over her.

"That was nice," she said. "The world seems full

of peaceful happiness to-night. I feel as if everybody loved me and felt gently toward me."

"Any one who does not has a quarrel brewing with me," laughed Isabel in return. "Oh, you rich girl! How many people back in our own world who have millions of dollars would exchange them all for that feeling you have just expressed! But it is a lazy feeling and it was putting you to sleep; I have something that I am sure will awaken you. Just wait here a moment."

She ran into their apartments and came out a minute later with a fine red rose and a note.

"Here is another drop of joy for your cup of happiness. It is a message that Izon gave me late this afternoon to deliver to you, and I could not find you. Personally, I think people have about reached the silly stage when they begin sending notes to each other after only an hour's absence."

Mariam, with a defiant little laugh at Isabel, had already greeted the rose with a kiss and was unfolding the note. She read it two or three times with rapt interest.

"Perfectly selfish," commented Isabel, eying her with mock jealousy. "Verse, I'll wager."

ZENO'S LITTLE GAME

"Yes, it is verse," admitted Mariam smiling, "and very sweet verse. Shall I read it to you?"

"Oh, I suppose I can endure it," retorted Isabel, and then to take away any apparent sting from her playful ungraciousness she slipped her arm under Mariam's head and, leaning her cheek against her cousin's, followed the moonlit words with her eyes as Mariam read them softly aloud.

"Dainty red Rose,
In Mariam's ear
Whisper my love,
My hope and fear.

"Take her this kiss.
Where petals meet,
Ask her to touch
Her lips so sweet.

"And then, so dear she is to me,
'T were Heav'n's bliss in thy place to be!"

"Heigh-ho," said Isabel with an exaggerated sigh when it was done. "I suppose that was the best he could do, but even then it was better than anything I can flaunt back at you. Nobody writes verses to me. I think I shall have to order a certain somebody to write some. Poor fellow! I can see him now, struggling over the task," and she laughed heartily at the picture of Black Eagle tearing his hair in the effort to write her a verse.

But her moods were unusually capricious to-night. The witchery of the moonlight seemed to have heightened within her all that was whimsical; and now she had a sudden longing to see Black Eagle again, perhaps to tease him and make up with him and then tease him again.

"Just to think," she charged, "that all on account of your note and your rose, which I suddenly remembered, I left a dear fellow who talks poetry even if he cannot write it. I'm going right back to him," and with a swirl she was gone.

She ran down to the seat where she had left Black Eagle, but he was not there, and she came back to the balcony. Mariam, still holding the rose to her cheek, had dropped asleep, and the smile that hovered upon her lips indicated that the old tradition as to moonlight slumber was true this time at least. Seen thus she was more lovely than she had ever appeared even to Isabel, whose admiration for Mariam knew no bounds. The moonlight, tinted to rosy softness by the red of the canyon walls, enveloped her in its mellow glow until she seemed to be the sleeping beauty of fable, waiting for the prince to awaken her. Hardly had the thought occured to Isabel when Izon appeared. Isabel, in the shadow, was not observed by him. He saw only Mariam, and kneeling by the side of the couch he smoothed the waving golden hair, very, very softly so that he might not disturb her. He gazed down adoringly upon the deeply fringed lashes and kissed delicately each blue-veined eyelid. The touch, though soft as the brush of a butterfly's wing, was still the electric touch of love, and it woke her at once.

"I was dreaming of you," she murmured.

The mischievous Isabel had no mischief in her now, and she shrank farther back into the shadow of a column. For once in her life she had come upon a moment too sacred for flippancy. The glory of the night was upon them, these two, in the prime of their youth and beauty.

"Come, Mariam," invited Izon, taking her hand and assisting her to arise from the couch. They strolled away, arm in arm, into the scented gardens, where the flowers exhaled intoxicating perfume. They

PRINCE IZON

wished that this night of rapture might be as endless as the caresses with which their bliss was sealed.

The sky was radiant with the magic lustre of the great white luminary hanging like a brilliant silver lamp in the blue dome above, its rays penetrating the shadows of the garden, lighting the grassy walks and converting into showers of jewels the sparkling jets of water from many fountains which cooled the air. The very songbirds seemed to be attuned to the mysterious bliss that quivered in the rosy moonlight, and rising above their ordinary notes they burst into a joyous ecstasy of melody.

Isabel, more thoughtful now than she had ever been, again went restlessly down to the garden, all idea of teasing Black Eagle gone. She fancied that she could be to him what Mariam was to Prince Izon, in the same gentle way. Once more she sought him in the garden, but, failing to find him, sat down upon the rustic chair. She had been there but a short time when a page swiftly crossed the space of moonlight which illuminated the sward. As the page approached she noted the extraordinary grace of the figure, which the costume displayed to perfection, and although the face was shadowed by the plumes of the cap, there was something about the carriage that she thought familiar. Approaching Isabel with a rush, the page seized her roughly and placed a hand over her mouth to stifle the screams which Isabel involuntarily sought to utter. A silvery laugh answered her struggle, and a voice she knew very well spoke to her.

"Why, Isabel, don't you know me?"

"Tequiepa!" cried Isabel in amazement, suddenly recognizing the tall, graceful girl who, next to Zaliza, was most in their company.

"At your service," repeated the girl merrily, and then sank her voice to a whisper. "I have been hunting all the shadows in the garden trying to find you, and I think I must have hidden from Black Eagle twenty times in the last half-hour. He is stalking around the garden and peering into the dark spots himself, so intently that I have been certain he would find me more than once. He seems to be looking for some one, and I think I can guess who that some one is. But now I want you to do me a favor. I am going to slip out of the lower gate and play a prank at home. With this cloak dropping from my shoulders, I am sure no one will detect me, especially so long as I keep in the shadows. The main gates, as you know, are all guarded. I don't want any one to know that I am doing this. The little gate is kept fastened and is guarded because only a certain few may use it, but it can be opened from the inside, and I want you to be down there and listen for my knock and let me in. Will you do this for me?"

"Why, certainly, my dear," replied Isabel cordially. "It is too beautiful a night to stay in," and she felt her face flushing.

"Oh, I know!" exclaimed the girl. "But you must promise me that when it is time to let me in you will slip away from that big fellow who wants to monopolize you."

Isabel laughed.

"I will arrange that for you," she promised. "I can quite understand why you do not want him to see you, even though he would be bound to agree with me that you are very pretty to look upon. Now run along and startle them all at home."

The girl started away reluctantly, for at once her conscience smote her for the duplicity she was practising. She had no intention of going home that night. She

ZENO'S LITTLE GAME

had been commissioned by Zeno to enact this part. She did not know what the outcome was to be, but she could not assume it to be an innocent one. She had been the recipient of nothing but kindness from both the girls, and like most of the Aztec beauties she was a creature of impulse. Turning suddenly she rushed back and threw her arms about Isabel.

"I want to tell you something!" she began. "I want to confess — "

At that moment the two girls were startled by a huge figure that stepped out of the shadows. A heavy hand swooped down upon Tequiepa's shoulder, jerking her violently away. The girl, a spirited descendant of a long line of warrior ancestors, made no outcry, but turning, faced him defiantly, clutching instinctively at her belt for the dagger that was not there. The next moment she would have been hurled to the ground had not Isabel started forward, crying,

"Stop, Black Eagle! It's Tequiepa!"

At the same moment, the girl's long hair, loosened by her cap having been knocked off, fell down in rippling waves to her knees, and Black Eagle stepped back in amazement.

PRINCE IZON

"Why, it is a girl!" he cried.

"Yes, and one who will punish you for this!" cried Tequiepa. "You shall know no moment more of peace in Ixtol. You have spoiled my plans and from now on your own will be balked at every turn — your schemes and those of your friends!"

Black Eagle only shrugged his shoulders and walked away. It was not in the blood of his race to quarrel with a woman. But though Tequiepa's words were but the idle threat of an angered girl, without authority or influence, they were prophetic. For from this night the four prisoners of Topeltzin were not to know one moment of security until the end, but were to be brought close under the broad black shadow that had so far only threatened them, and were even to be chilled by the near wings of grim Death itself!

CHAPTER XVIII
DELIVERANCE AT HAND

THIS was to be a night of events. Tequiepa's encounter with Black Eagle had checked her repentance. She allowed Isabel to do up her hair, and remembering that after all Zeno was of the priesthood and might have urgent reasons of state for his action, departed after receiving Isabel's repeated promise to let her in at the lower gate just before midnight. Isabel, left alone, now followed the direction taken by Black Eagle, with a fair certainty of where she would find him. She remembered a sheltered nook in the far end of the terrace where Mariam and herself had spent hours in seclusion and, turning into this nook, she found Black Eagle, but with him was a tall, dark-cowled stranger clad in the garb of an Aztec priest. She was about to turn away when Black Eagle called her. She came up at once.

"Father," he said, "this is one of the maidens found with Izon. Isabel," turning to her gravely, "this is Father Zolcoma, the spiritual leader of the Pearl City, who has risked much in coming to us to guide us to freedom."

The tall stranger turned and as he did so the cowl slipped from his head, revealing his patriarchal visage crowned with silvery hair. Isabel reverently bent her head under his outstretched hand.

"Black Eagle has told us of your devotion to Prince Izon," she said, "and we are grateful to share in the benefit of the work that is being done for him. Have you finished the tunnel?"

"Yes, but speak almost in a whisper," he cautioned. "We have completed the small passageway upon which we have been working ever since we heard of Prince Izon's capture, but it did not come out where we wished it, and is only high enough at this part to crawl through upon hands and knees. You will have to climb up to get into the passageway. It will be very difficult and very dangerous, I fear, but we do not dare take time to make it larger."

"I am sure, father," replied Isabel, "that you will find us ready to undergo any hardship."

"Spoken in the right spirit, my daughter," said

DELIVERANCE AT HAND

Father Zolcoma. "Go now and find the prince and the other member of your party."

"The other member of the party is to be the princess some time," Isabel informed him, "and I have no doubt that the two will be glad for this and certain other services that a priest can offer them."

She had laid her hand affectionately upon Black Eagle's arm as she spoke, and Father Zolcoma smiled as he saw the chieftain unconsciously patting the hand.

"It looks to me as if I should be very busily occupied with all four of you," he replied, "but as I would much rather officiate at a double wedding than at a quadruple death, I expect some one had better hasten to bring our friends here."

"They are in the garden somewhere, Black Eagle," directed Isabel. "The last I saw of them they were near the labyrinth. You had best go there for them first. May we all go together or shall we separate and hunt for them?"

"Nay, I must stay here," replied Father Zolcoma. "It will not do for me to be found in the garden. This spot is very near and quite accessible to the tunnel branch that we have opened into this place. If Black Eagle can find our friends without our assistance we will wait here for him."

Black Eagle was already striding away and Father Zolcoma looked after him with kindly eyes.

"He is a splendid man," he said, admiring the broad shoulders and sturdy swing. "He is the kind we want in the White City. You seem to be perfectly happy, both of you. I presume you are well treated."

"We are surrounded with every comfort and given entire liberty," replied Isabel, "except that of course we cannot leave the Red City. I would find life very pleasant here only that I miss the church and am troubled by the doom that hangs over Prince Izon."

Father Zolcoma shuddered.

"I fear you do not understand just how dreadful that doom is," he replied. "Owing to a desperate battle that resulted, long ago, from the practice of the pagans in kidnapping for the sacrifice their Christian brethren who had business in Ixtol, a treaty was made to the effect that no inhabitant of either city could ever enter the other on pain of capture and death, the only alternative being the renunciation of his own faith for that of his

DELIVERANCE AT HAND

captors, and this provision resulted in the practice, by the pagans, of ambush and capture anywhere on neutral territory. In an evil hour Prince Izon resolved to seek a wife in the outer world, obeying a misty tradition which links a sun-haired maiden to the line of the Montezumas, which is thereby to become imperishable. The tradition is probably an offshoot from the same belief which made the Aztecs ready to welcome the first white man as the long-expected god from the east. But be that as it may, our romantic prince was impressed by it, and, after brooding a long time, he resolved, against my earnest advice, to set out with a party of nobles to seek the ideal love that his fancy had conjured. You know the rest. In a few days, he met you and Mariam and deemed his quest ended. What you do not know is that Topeltzin, through his spies, knew of this venture, and at once saw his chance to not only score a great triumph but to secure an exalted victim for his altar. He instantly despatched a strong force to capture Izon. They succeeded, but they did not anticipate the capture of two young girls also. You were therefore separated and Izon given the alternative provided for in the treaty, either to adjure his Christianity or to be sacrificed. In his cruel dilemma he had but one choice, feeling responsible for your safety. He accepted the role of the victim, hoping that rescue in some way or other would come."

"Yes, we know much of all this. Mariam, I believe, even knows, at least partly, the sort of sacrifice that awaits him. Her father, with whose deep researches into Aztec history you are doubtless familiar, at one time gave her some inkling of it, but she will not speak of it. She says it is too horrible."

"It is," answered Father Zolcoma. "Nothing like it was ever practised by any other nation in the world. At the time of the conquest by Cortez it was a national custom. Some time before the sacrifice, a captive, distinguished for his personal beauty and without a blemish upon his body, was selected to represent the deity, Tezcatlipoca. He was received within the city with all the honors of a god, and was arrayed in splendid dress and regaled with incense and a profusion of honors. When he went abroad the crowd prostrated themselves before him as being the actual representative of their deity. He thus lived a life of luxury until a short time before the sacrifice, when three beautiful girls were selected for

DELIVERANCE AT HAND

his wives and with them he lived in voluptuousness, feasted at the banquets of the nobles and the ruler who paid him all the honors of the divinity, until at last the fatal day of the sacrifice arrived. The term of his short-lived glories was at an end. He was stripped of his fine apparel and marched up to the summit of the temple, where he was received by the priests who led him to the sacrificial stone, a huge block of jasper with its upper surface convex. On this he was laid, the priests securing his head and limbs while the high priest dexterously opened his side with a knife and tore out his heart. The minister of death first held this up to the sun, then cast it at the feet of the statue of the deity, while the multitude below prostrated themselves in humble adoration."

Father Zolcoma ceased and as Isabel imagined the dreadful scene, a thrill of horror convulsed her.

"Terrible!" she exclaimed. "And Izon knows all this?"

"Undoubtedly."

"And he could escape it by embracing this pagan worship?"

"Easily. They would be glad to have him do so.

PRINCE IZON

The people would be overjoyed to have him resume his hereditary leadership, although I fancy Topeltzin would rather have him led to the top of the teocolli. Prince Izon, however, will never renounce his faith."

"And he had only to do this to save himself?"

"He is a hero," responded Father Zolcoma. "The only temptation that could assail him, the thought that by embracing the paganism of his forefathers he could save you and the girl he loves, must have been a tremendous strain upon him, but now it is happily almost over. If everything goes well, within another hour we shall be out of Topeltzin's clutches and safe from all pursuit."

They were disturbed by the tread of a sentry down the path. Father Zolcoma quickly pulled forward his cowl, and the sentry, recognizing Isabel and seeing her in company with one who was apparently an Aztec priest, passed on without so much as turning his head. But he reported the incident to his superior and in a short time several pairs of eyes were watching the grotto from outside places of hiding. Father Zolcoma smiled as the watch passed by, and cast a look of disdain at the row of flaming torches which had dotted the topmost

DELIVERANCE AT HAND

cliff since Black Eagle's escape and reëntry by that route.

"Futile, all in vain, those gleaming torches," he exulted. "We are going under and not over that cliff, friend Topeltzin."

They sat down in the little nook and conversed in low tones for a time, until Father Zolcoma began to get uneasy. It was now nearly half-past eleven and every additional moment of delay meant additional danger of discovery. Isabel, at Father Zolcoma's suggestion, went into the grounds to hunt Mariam and Izon. She did not go near the labyrinth, remembering that Black Eagle had been sent there. If she had penetrated its depths, however, she would have found Black Eagle lost in its maze, wandering around and around, not daring to call out and rendered more liable to error in direction by reason of his haste.

At the end of a twenty-minute search she found Izon. He informed her that Mariam had just gone to her apartments. He was overjoyed to know that the tunnel was completed and that Father Zolcoma was waiting to show them the way. Sending him up to join the venerable priest, Isabel hurried back to the palace to summon Mariam. She passed the little gate on her way and an impatient knocking reminded her suddenly of her promise to Tequiepa. Hastily opening the gate, she enabled the page to enter.

"Pardon me," she said. "I am in haste!"

She made a direct line through the lower garden at a rapid pace, the page following close behind her. It was just at this moment that Black Eagle, finding himself in one of the outer convolutions of the maze, and despairing of getting through it, seized the knife at his belt and began to savagely hack and hew at the hedge which formed the walls of the labyrinth. Making an opening he squeezed himself hastily through it, scratching his hands and tearing his clothing. Going toward the palace, he saw, mounting the outside steps leading to the floor upon which were the women's apartments, the flutter of a white gown, and assuming it to be either Mariam or Isabel, he strode toward the palace. It was Isabel, closely followed by the page. She hastened back through the corridor, the columns of which cast deep shadows from the few flaring lights that were suspended from its ceiling. Just as she reached the door of her

DELIVERANCE AT HAND

own and Mariam's apartments, the page caught up with her and placed a hand upon her shoulder.

"Isabel," said the page in a low tone, "don't you know me?"

"Zeno!" she exclaimed.

"Yes, my queen," he replied in the same subdued tone. "It is Zeno."

"What do you mean by this masquerade and by addressing me in that way?" Isabel demanded.

"You should know what it means!" he replied extending his arms. "Surely you have seen my love for you! From the moment you appeared among us I adored you!"

"You must have lost your senses!" she exclaimed. "I have but barely spoken with you some half-dozen times."

"That was sufficient," he interrupted. "In this land and clime it requires but a word, but a look, to start the flame of passion. It needed but a glance from your sparkling eyes to wield the spell that is now upon me. Isabel, I cannot live without you! You must give me at least a word of hope."

"Enough of this!" said Isabel impatiently. "You amaze me, for I have been told you are engaged to Zaliza. Leave me at once or I shall tell her of this treachery."

"Zaliza," he echoed, raising his voice. "What is she? You alone possess my heart! You, enchantress that you are, with a beauty so radiant that all others pale before it; you who have so captivated me that I have braved the fury of Zaliza, yes, would brave even death itself to meet you here; you will tell me that I may hope, for death will be preferable to life without you!"

He seized her as he finished and, despite her resistance, drew her towards him.

"Then it will be death!" said a stern voice, and the next moment the powerful arms of Black Eagle had grasped him.

In a moment they were struggling fiercely, but in silence, although the young priest was as a child in the hands of the chieftain. Suddenly, with a mighty exertion, Black Eagle threw him across his shoulder, and rushing to a balcony at the end of the corridor, hurled him over, shrieking, to the garden below!

CHAPTER XIX

THE FIGHT IN THE GROTTO

ZENO'S carefully constructed drama, even had it come through without mishap, would have failed to impress the audience for whom it had been prepared. While his discomfiture was being accomplished, two figures, muffled in cloaks, had been concealed behind the curtains that hung before the doorway leading into Zaliza's apartments, just opposite Isabel and Mariam's, and as Zeno's shriek rang out Zaliza clutched Topeltzin's arm. She was breathless for a moment from the excitement of it all, and then, calming, she was full of disdain. She could scarcely restrain her scorn until Isabel, after a hasty whispered direction to Black Eagle, had entered her apartments and the chieftain had hurried out of the corridor.

"Fool!" she exclaimed. "It served him right!"

"Zeno," replied Topeltzin, dryly, "could no more help being born a fool than you could help being born beautiful. The gods regulate these matters to their own taste."

"Where is the prince?" asked Zaliza impatiently. "You told me I should see him here. My lord, if I do not presently possess him, you shall wonder at what dagger and poison may do among your fine prisoners of state!" and her great black eyes gleamed dangerously.

"There is some misunderstanding, and evidently he will not be here," replied Topeltzin evasively, looking askance upon this fiery beauty, whom he believed quite capable of carrying out any threat. "By Tezcat! What strength that Indian has!"

"He is magnificent!" she answered. "But allow me to retire, my lord. I have had my fill of incidents to-night."

The high priest stepped into the full light of the corridor.

"Then you have no qualms of jealousy in seeing Zeno make love to another woman?" he observed, smiling.

"Jealousy and contempt of the one man never live together in the same bosom," she answered, entering her own doorway. "Good-night, my lord."

As Topeltzin went to his rooms, he was unusually

FIGHT IN THE GROTTO

thoughtful. Up to this time he had scarcely recognized the existence of Black Eagle, but now he was suddenly impressed with him as a possible factor in his plans, and as a possible bar to their fulfilment.

He had scarcely reached the room, that was the centre of the spider-web upon the filaments of which he kept such sensitive tentacles, when a violent drumming assailed his ears. Hastily responding, the first word that he heard startled him out of the calm imperturbability with which he was usually cloaked.

"What!" he exclaimed. "Repeat that!"

He listened intently, frowning deeply and drumming upon the table with nervous fingers.

"Summon the guards immediately, and hold them assembled for me!" he ordered, and as he hastily left the apartment he muttered, "There will be several new arrivals to-night in Zetler [the Aztec hell]."

In the meantime, Isabel had found Mariam in the midst of her attendants just being prepared for retiring, but Mariam was overjoyed to slip into outer garments of fabric coarse enough to withstand rough travel, and hurry with Isabel to the garden. It was a happy yet anxious quintet that met in the grotto into which the

PRINCE IZON

workmen from the White City had tunnelled. As soon as they had assembled Father Zolcoma ascended, by means of a ladder, to the mouth of the tunnel and explained carefully that it would be necessary for them to crawl on hands and knees for at least two hundred feet before they could stand erect.

"Remember, my children, that the moments are precious," he charged.

"Waste no time in discussion as to precedence. To avoid such folly I now appoint Isabel to follow me, then Mariam, then Prince Izon, with Black Eagle as the last. He must draw up the ladder after him."

Isabel put her feet upon the ladder to follow him but at that moment there were hoarse cries and the sound of rushing feet outside, and then Topeltzin, followed by a company of his guards, burst into the grotto. A fatal hour had been lost in hunting Mariam and Izon, and in that time the plot had been discovered and reported to the high priest by the spies that had been watching the grotto. Topeltzin was furious, but the chief object of his wrath was not the prince nor Black Eagle nor the girls, but Father Zolcoma, the only enemy whose power and ability he feared. Dashing Isabel

FIGHT IN THE GROTTO

aside, he sprang after Father Zolcoma, who had paused on the ladder. Topeltzin reached up to grasp him, but Black Eagle caught the Aztec ruler by his robe and jerked him so violently that he fell backwards. The guards were upon Black Eagle in a moment, and bore him down by weight of numbers. Izon plunged in to help his friend, but he, too, was overpowered for a moment. It was a perilous time, but the fight was not to be so easily won. Father Zolcoma, instead of retreating through the tunnel as he might have done, jumped off the ladder, and in a moment more it was seen why he had done so. There followed him, swarming down, some score of his followers who had been brought along to aid in case any surprise of the sort should occur.

The girls, cowering back in the corner of the grotto and unable to get out of the narrow doorway, were forced to witness the desperate hand-to-hand conflict that now ensued between Topeltzin's guard and the followers of Father Zolcoma. Black Eagle and Prince Izon were upon their feet fighting furiously, and in the *mêlée* towered Topeltzin, his eyes flashing with anger and white flecks of foam upon his lips. The girls were surprised to see Captain Helox among the soldiers

PRINCE IZON

of Topeltzin, no longer in the garb of an officer but as one of the common guards. They saw that once he threw himself between Izon and a spear that was poised at him, himself pinning Izon to the ground. Starting forward they saw that Helox, while apparently struggling with Izon, was whispering something in his ear. They saw him, at another time, himself strike a surreptitious blow that disabled the right arm of a guard bent on strangling Black Eagle as he was held by four others, and though it was but slightly that Helox could aid their party, the girls felt comforted in the thought that there were friends near, surrounded even as they were by such enemies.

Izon and Black Eagle and the soldiers from the White City fought fiercely, and the militant Father Zolcoma did his full share, but they were fighting against heavy odds, for fresh relays of guards poured in from the reserves at the palace, and in the end they were all overpowered except Father Zolcoma, who was seized with apparent ferocity by Captain Helox and dragged by him into the darkness without. Half a dozen of the palace guards would never fight again. Prince Izon with torn garments, and Black Eagle with

FIGHT IN THE GROTTO

an ugly cut upon his shoulder, were led away, and the bound soldiers from the Pearl City, all except three who had been slain, were driven to the dungeons below the palace. It was easy to conjecture their fate.

Topeltzin, pausing to take breath after the final victorious struggle, scrutinized his prisoners with grim satisfaction until all at once his brow clouded and the fierce anger came back again to his face.

"Zolcoma!" he gasped. "Where is he? By Texcat! You dogs, if you 've let him escape — !"

Without finishing the threat he immediately despatched guards to scour the garden. Innumerable lights, flaring and smoking, turned the moonlit darkness into yellow day. Scores of guards searched every nook and cranny of the garden, but without success, while the girls were sent to their quarters and Amazon guards were set to keep them close prisoners, for the time being at least. An hour elapsed, but the swarm of searchers could not find Father Zolcoma. They did, however, find Captain Helox outside the gates returning to the palace, on the road leading to Luxtol, and they brought him, defiantly silent, before Topeltzin to explain his strange actions.

CHAPTER XX

THE REVOLT OF ZILPAN

TIRED but not discouraged, Father Zolcoma reached the Pearl City, and although dawn was just breaking he sought no rest, but at once called Lord Toltec, Father Orlozo, and the other leaders into consultation — first telling them the details of the unfortunate night's events. "I now suggest," he concluded, "that we call at the palace and tell the Queen Mother, Lady Zulaza, just how matters stand. It will add to her burden of grief but we all know that she is a woman of courage and I crave her advice."

The home of the descendants of Montezuma was worthy of the race, although the refinements of Christianity had modified some of the luxuries of the Chepultepec palace. Izon's father had died when he was a child, but his mother had proven herself admirably fitted for the regency and the task of bringing up the prince until he should reach his majority.

When the councillors had reached the audience room

THE REVOLT OF ZILPAN

they were welcomed with quiet dignity. The source of Prince Izon's comeliness was apparent in his mother's noble cast of features. A crown of silvery hair surmounted a high-caste face, and although her eyes flashed through unshed tears as Father Zolcoma repeated his story, her firm red-lipped mouth expressed unflinching determination.

"Of course," the father concluded, "this will shorten Izon's time, and knowing the malignity of Topeltzin as well as we all do, you will agree with me that the difficulty of rescuing all four of the prisoners is quadrupled. Topeltzin will now try to keep them separated so that any effort to rescue all will be four times liable to detection."

"I agree with you entirely," said Lord Toltec. "Have you thought of any other plan?"

"Not for the four," answered Father Zolcoma sadly. "It seems utterly impossible. But I have thought of a plan whereby Izon may possibly escape alone."

"He will never consent," cried Father Orlozo.

"He must consent," said Lord Toltec sternly. "In the first place it would be a useless sacrifice of himself and his friends to insist on being liberated together, a thing which after the failure last night is impracticable. In the second place, his companions will not necessarily suffer by being left behind because they have made many friends among the nobility of Ixtol who will stand between them and Topeltzin; and in the third place, he is needed here. He is the best and most progressive ruler Luxtol has ever had."

"Yes," replied Father Zolcoma, "and it would be a terrible blow to our civilization and our Christianity to have the pagans of Ixtol triumph over us in this vital matter, but I am afraid Father Orlozo is right."

"I will lay upon him the command of the people," answered Lord Toltec, "and you, father, the command of the church, and you, my lady, the command of an honored mother; this will enable us to send a message that no son of the Montezumas dare disobey."

A grave silence ensued. The door of the council chamber opened, and Professor Raymon came in. The members of the assemblage looked at one another significantly. Professor Raymon caught the glance and turned toward the door.

"I beg your pardon," he said, "I called at your house and was told you were absent. Am I intruding?"

THE REVOLT OF ZILPAN

"By no means," replied Father Zolcoma; "come and join us. You have a right, a father's right, to sit in this deliberation." He then presented him to the Queen Mother.

Lord Toltec said, "We are trying to devise some new plan to rescue the prince."

He emphasized the word "prince" with meaning, and Professor Raymon, gazing from one to the other of the grave faces surrounding the table, slowly comprehended.

"Then the others — " he faltered.

"The others will have to take their chances," replied Lord Toltec. "It seems a hard decision, but there is no other way. After we have rescued the prince we will make another attempt to take his companions, finally resorting to force, if need be. If we attempted force to rescue Izon, however, they would kill him before they would let him go."

"There is only one stumbling block," said Lady Zulaxa, "and that will be the refusal of Izon to leave the others behind."

"You need have no fear for that," said Professor Raymon. His face was pale but his voice was firm.

PRINCE IZON

"I can answer for the girls, and I know Black Eagle's brave nature too well to doubt him for a moment. Leave that part of the programme to them."

"We certainly thank you," said Father Zolcoma, with a sigh of relief.

"I hope, father, that you may not be disappointed," said Lady Zulaxa; "but I know Izon so well — know how determined he is when once a course is fixed in his mind, that I have doubts. You have reasons for agreeing with me, as witness our unavailing efforts to dissuade him from taking this venture into the main canyon, which has caused all this calamity."

Before Father Zolcoma could reply, one of the acolytes hastily entered the room. He seemed much excited.

"The man Zilpan, whom we found in the north tower in mind communication with Topeltzin, claims conversion and desires earnestly to see the council," he announced.

"Bring him here," Lord Toltec directed, and in a short time Zilpan was shown into the room. His eyes were deep with suffering, his face was haggard.

"I renounce Tezcatlipoca and all his priests! I de-

THE REVOLT OF ZILPAN

nounce Topeltzin and all his crew!" His voice trembled with passion. "My poor Azra! Topeltzin keeps her a prisóner in her tower, and every day he sends Tepultac to her and is trying to force her to receive his attentions. He has forbidden her to communicate with me in any way, but over that he has no power. So long as she has life she can send out her thought to me, and no force can prevent it. But listen! The means of communication that he so carefully opened up between the two cities is still open, and I am going to use his own machine against him. Heretofore he utilized Azra and myself as a steady flow of news from the Pearl City to the Red. The flow will keep up, but now it will be the other way. All the news will come from the Red City to the Pearl. Here is what I am able to tell you to-day." He swayed slightly, and caught the table for support. Professor Raymon hastily drew up a chair for him. A glass of water revived him somewhat. "The festival of the sacrifice is announced for to-morrow night!" he exclaimed.

Father Zolcoma started.

"So soon!" he cried. "That means that the day after, Prince Izon must ascend the teocolli. It means that our attempts to rescue him will have cut his life much shorter if we do not finally save him."

Zilpan held up his hand for silence. He was breathing with difficulty and was anxious to deliver his message while he had strength.

"Captain Helox," he announced, "is imprisoned, and now the captain of the guards is Gautemotzin."

Again Father Zolcoma lifted up his head in quick dismay.

"Gautemotzin!" he exclaimed. "That degenerate descendant of the most brilliant warrior in Aztec history, the most inveterate hater of Christianity in all the canyon; a giant in stature and a tiger in ferocity! This bodes ill for us."

"The two girl captives," went on Zilpan, "are allowed their liberty, but now they are always attended by stalwart women attendants. They are not allowed to be with Black Eagle and Prince Izon, except when so attended. Two soldiers each have been set to guard Black Eagle and Prince Izon night and day, with orders under pain of death not to let them out of their sight, nor to allow them to engage in any whispered conferences."

THE REVOLT OF ZILPAN

For a long time not another word was spoken. Only the labored breathing of Zilpan broke the silence.

"This festival," said Father Zolcoma thoughtfully, "will of course be a masked revel, as is customary. Can we trust Azra?" he asked suddenly.

"With life itself," Zilpan's voice had a new ring. The mention of Azra was like a draught of old wine to him.

"Does she know that you have resolved to turn your allegiance to the Christians?"

"She does."

"And will she do likewise?"

Zilpan squared his shoulders proudly.

"My religion is her religion," he answered. "We have Topeltzin caught in his own meshes. Tepultac has not fallen in love with Azra, for the tragic reason that his heart is still with Zalid, his mate, whom the insatiate and monstrous desires of Topeltzin would not spare, and who died by her own hand. Tepultac lives only for revenge, and it was but yesterday that he made a startling confession of Christianity to Azra and vowed himself to our service. Helox knew of this, but Tepultac preferred to be an unknown spy. He wants to be an instrument in the downfall of Topeltzin. He is free to come and go. Topeltzin is bending every energy to make Azra forget me and accept Tepultac for ends of his own, and so, for a time, we can deceive him."

"Good!" cried Father Zolcoma. "Perhaps through all this we may yet save our good children. In the meantime convey in some way to Prince Izon that on the night of the festival we will have a strong armed force concealed outside the north gate of the Red City wall. Have Black Eagle and Prince Izon, if possible, elude their body guards long enough to exchange costumes after they have been seen and recognized conspicuously about the grounds. The two can then manœuvre to get themselves and their four guards in a more or less secluded portion of the gardens, and Black Eagle may then engage in a pretended attempt at escape. All four of the guards will pursue him, thinking that he is Prince Izon. Izon then, in Black Eagle's costume, must run for the gate. When he arrives near enough, he must call to our soldiers, who can break open the gate and easily overpower the guard. If, in the meantime, the girls and Black Eagle can get down to the gate, we may be able to get them all away, but it must be under-

THE REVOLT OF ZILPAN

stood, first, last, and all the time, that every interest must give way before the safety of the prince."

At this the council arose, Lady Zulaza dismissing them with impressive dignity and concluding with an imperious gesture, she cried,

"If this plan fails, then I beg of you to see that a weapon is conveyed to Izon so that before he ascends the teocolli, or after he does, he can defend himself to the last, and if he must die, it will not be the death of the shameful sacrifice, but the glorious death of a warrior prince!"

CHAPTER XXI

THE NIGHT BEFORE THE FESTIVAL

THE Red City bustled with preparations for the approaching festival, when Izon's final decision must be made, when his three wives would be presented to him, and when he would be given the choice to forswear his God or die, and the holiday spirit drove from the minds of the people all thoughts of mercy, even their hereditary love for the Prince of the House of Montezuma. The regularity with which the great sacrifice had been performed for ages had had its natural reflex upon the character of the people and the slightest excitement, no matter from what cause, whetted their blood-thirsty appetites. Moreover, with the accession of Topeltzin to power, a great wave of moral degeneracy had swept over the city; its denizens were given over to riotous pleasure; brawls and even murders were of frequent occurrence; the honor of its women and the integrity of its men were at the lowest ebb in the history of these people, whom Cortez had found honest and gentle

BEFORE THE FESTIVAL

and in many ways more refined than the Spaniards, with the tremendous single exception of this bloody custom. Now girls and young men, half drunken and wearing chaplets of flowers, were dancing and singing in the streets day and night in anticipation of the great festival.

Isabel and Mariam were terrified by the mad atmosphere that pervaded even the palace. Young Tequiepa, the girl whose beauty had so impressed them, the same one who had enacted the part of a page at Zeno's bidding, shocked them by coming through a corridor of the palace, half tipsy, with her arm about the neck of the big, ugly Gautemotzin. Seeing the two girls, he dropped Tequiepa and made a dash for them. The liquor that was surging in his veins had taken away his self-control entirely, and had it not been for the fortunate appearance of Topeltzin upon the scene, he must surely have offered them some indignity. As it was, the girls were so frightened that they were glad to have their women guards with them, and now they seldom ventured from their apartments, but sat, alone and miserable, trembling with apprehension. Black Eagle and Izon they never saw except at a distance. They could feel the toils tightening about them, and for the first time since their captivity they began to realize their position in all its horror.

In this juncture Tepultac was the only ray of hope. He had his own good and sufficient reasons for loathing Topeltzin from the bottom of his heart, and Azra through sympathy had secured an ascendency over him which was in itself a force tremendous enough to drive him to great deeds. The very Christianity which these three students of Topeltzin had embraced was with them a wild, savage thing which they by no means understood. All three had suddenly turned to this mighty force for vengeance, and not until more peaceful times, when under the benign teachings of Father Zolcoma, could they be brought to understand the divine messages of mercy that Christianity upholds. Tepultac managed to secure more than one quiet talk with Izon and Black Eagle, and the guards that were placed over these two did not suspect him. He was of the priesthood, and known to be in close touch with Topeltzin. It was through him, then, that Father Zolcoma was able to convey to Prince Izon the dread word of command which humbled him to sway of duty to the people of his fathers, and to instruct him and Black Eagle in the parts

BEFORE THE FESTIVAL

they must take in the attempt the prince was to make to escape through change of costume.

It was through his connivance, too, that on the night before the festival the four were able to meet in a secluded spot in the palace grounds, for he got the guards intoxicated, a matter that was very easy to accomplish in this time of rioting and intemperance, and he drugged their liquor so they lay asleep not a dozen paces away from where the sad-hearted little quartet met to discuss their plans. Tepultac addressed them earnestly:

"If Prince Izon does not escape to-morrow night," he said, "he will ascend the teocolli. At the same time the soldiers of the White City will march to the gates of the Red and be ready to storm them when the ceremonies of the sacrifice begin. To make this attack before that time will be out of the question on account of Topeltzin's announcement that any such attempt would cause Izon's instant execution. There is only one place where Izon will be safe from such a fate, and that will be on top of the teocolli where there is not sufficient room for a very large number. At the time for the sacrifice, all the people of the Red City that can crowd in will be at the base of the teocolli and, of course, will be unarmed. All the armed forces of the Red City will be at the gates to repel the White City army. Azra from her tower will watch the teocolli. As soon as the sacrificial ceremonies begin, she will communicate the fact to Zilpan who will be with the Pearl City soldiers, and the battle will begin. If the Christian forces succeed in storming the gates and entering the city they will surround the unarmed multitude in the plaza and hold them in check until Izon, Black Eagle, and yourselves descend from the teocolli."

"Ourselves?" Isabel repeated, wonderingly.

"Exactly, for you two girls are to take part, and be with the prince, if possible. You are to ascend the temple at dawn and conceal yourselves, for it is from there only that you will have any opportunity of escape. If the attempt to escape from the garden fails, then the top of the teocolli must be your last stand and only possible hope. Black Eagle's part then comes in and it will be one of extreme danger."

Isabel paled, and turning to Black Eagle swiftly, put her hand upon his arm. He patted the hand, a caress now customary with him.

"Never mind!" he exclaimed. "I will accept the

BEFORE THE FESTIVAL

chance gladly and you need not fear that, in case Prince Izon gets away, they will take me for the sacrifice. By the time they get through fighting with me I will be no fit subject for the ceremony, as the victim must be without a scar or blemish."

One of the guards upon the ground began to stir uneasily.

"We may talk no more," said Tepultac. "I have one more message from Father Zolcoma to you. These are his own words," and sinking his voice to a gravely solemn tone, he held his hands extended over them. " 'May the blessing of the Father, the Son, and the Holy Spirit rest upon you and guide you in all these things and lead you to safety and happiness!'

"Remember, even if the attempt to-morrow night fails, the day of the sacrifice is Sunday, and our Lord will surely not allow it to be desecrated in such a horrible manner; your Christian brethren in the Pearl City will be praying for you."

The guard, who had been turning restlessly, now arose to his elbow. He was not looking toward them but out over the canyon, dazed, trying to collect his wits.

"Hurry," said Tepultec. "Make your adieus brief and let us go."

He turned his head and his eyes filled with tears as the young people embraced, and then quietly separated.

After they had gone a sixth member of the little conclave crept out from amid the shrubbery where he had been crouching, concealed, and he also stole away through the shadows. It was Zeno, who now hurried to report to his master. He walked slowly and with a quite perceptible limp. He had been most subdued since that night when Black Eagle had thrown him over the balcony. The branches of a tree had checked his fall, so that he had only sustained some ugly scratches and sprains, but even a greater change had come to the inner Zeno. He was torn and anguished by a dozen conflicting emotions, so that he scarcely knew his own mind.

CHAPTER XXII

THE MASKED FESTIVAL

THE night of the festival had arrived, bringing with it a height of madness upon which Topeltzin looked down, like the evil genius of the whole revel, from one of the many ornate roof parapets.

Without the palace walls, in the plazas, the sound of feasting and carousing from the assembled thousands sounded like the distant roar of a cataract. Immense barbecues had been made for the populace, and up to the glaring open spaces had come, grotesquely masked, hordes of creatures that were wont to shun the light. They were everywhere, seared but still seething within from the passions that consumed them, the veritable pestilential spirit of the poisonous decay that had fallen, upon this branch of the once great Aztec race. Here arose, side by side, shrieks of merriment and shrieks of terror, as the daughters of the more wholesome middle classes found themselves seized by ghouls of that unspeakable underworld that inhabited the lower canyon close to the rushing waters, veritable Troglodytes who, unable or unwilling to build shelters, found refuge in the lower caves amid frightful abominations. But for all this Topeltzin had little thought. His mind was bent more upon the vast palace gardens, where all was beauty and light.

The rich moonlight, glorified, as always, by the tinted walls of the canyon, was reinforced by the many brilliant lights that flamed and twinkled among the trees and that sent their streaming radiance from the mouths of the grottos. Music filled the air at frequent intervals, while everywhere, upon the winding paths, scattered over the sward, ascending and descending the steps, and passing into and out of the luxurious caverns, were handsomely robed maskers, the men distinguished by waving plumes of quetzal feathers, such as only the nobility were permitted to wear, while the golden ornaments, crusted with jewels, glittering upon glowing breasts and necks and arms and in the hair of fair women, produced a kaleidoscopic effect which highly elated the prime mover of all this pageant.

"All for you, Tezcatlipoca!" Topeltzin exclaimed, gazing towards the teocolli, on whose summit in the

THE MASKED FESTIVAL

bright moonlight could be seen the colossal statue of the deity. "Behold the glorification of the eve of your great feast to-morrow! Behold the seething caldron of human passion that I — I alone have set aflame in your honor!"

He turned and passed down the steps that led to the garden, to plunge himself into this vertex of blind, thoughtless pleasure.

But, if the scene affected him thus, two of the watchers, standing in a balcony overlooking the gardens, were delighted and charmed with the spectacle, even in spite of the dread significance of it all. It was the most brilliant and animated scene that they had ever looked upon or imagined, and they were young enough to enjoy every new effect of the ever changing color scheme. Suddenly, Mariam caught sight of a tall figure, passing the flood of light that streamed from a grotto, a figure that glittered with gold and flashed with gems from head to foot.

"See, Isabel!" she cried with a thrill in her voice. "See, even in that great throng, how easily Izon stands out far above them all!"

Isabel, whose hand was resting lightly upon Mariam's shoulder, gripped it with an involuntary gesture of sympathetic admiration as she noted the majestic figure which Mariam had pointed out. Izon was accoutred in the same magnificent costume he had worn upon the day of his triumphal entry into the Red City, and wherever he went heads were prostrated. It was a curious anomaly, this reverence paid to a man who within a short time, the same people would see most ruthlessly butchered.

Another tall figure approached from the opposite direction, and it was Isabel's turn to claim the need of admiration due her own knight.

"That one is mine!" she boasted. "Except for Izon's wonderful head-dress I do not believe there is an inch of difference in their height. They are grand, both of them, perfectly splendid!"

Involuntarily the two girls clasped each other's hands, as the two men in the garden stopped to converse. Black Eagle, in the shining armor of a Spanish cavalier, dating from the time of Cortez, seemed colossal, and they looked so striking that every neck was craned as the throngs, in passing, finished making their deep obeisances.

THE MASKED FESTIVAL

The girls turned to each other with glances of smiling understanding as they saw that Izon and Black Eagle kept their places for some time, and that they had their visors raised as they talked. Their plan was in operation. They were endeavoring to be identified with their costumes by as many people as possible. The girls noted also that behind each two stalwart maskers were stationed. The inordinate breadth of their shoulders and the taut hanging of their arms betrayed them as guards. Presently one of the guards twitched Black Eagle diffidently by the elbow and spoke to him, then the men lowered their visors and passed on.

"Come," said Mariam, "it is time for us to go into the garden. We have work to do."

Isabel sighed deeply.

"I suppose it is weak to confess how much I dread that ordeal," she said. "Even since we have been standing here the increase of recklessness has been clearly apparent. The crowds are moving quicker, the voices are growing louder and shriller, the laughter is growing more abandoned. There is no order or safety in this dreadful place! Look, Mariam! Look at that, and then think into what a maelstrom we must go!"

PRINCE IZON

A shriek had at that moment rung out. A young girl had been snatched up from her companions and was now being borne away, screaming and struggling, upon the shoulder of a stalwart ruffian in red and green. To her cry for help only heartless laughter responded. A slight cavalier in yellow, however, sprang after her, short sword in hand. There was a brief struggle, the clash of sword upon sword. The shrill sounds in that vicinity suddenly changed their tone, then ceased abruptly. The fellow in green and red sank to the ground. The girl walked away supported on the arm of the slight cavalier. Presently two of the servants of the palace emerged from the crowd, bearing the fallen reveller on a stretcher, and in a moment more the mad throng, shrieking and laughing as before, was pressing on in the erratic tenor of its way. The incident was already forgotten.

Mariam had paled, but now she took up her mask to adjust it.

"We must forget these things," she said calmly. "We are needed."

They were about to turn into the corridor when a masked man stepped hastily up to them, limping as

THE MASKED FESTIVAL

he walked. The girls were surprised to see that their own guards were not present. Four of the stalwart women who had been detailed to watch over them had been just inside the balcony entrance. The newcomer noted their questioning glance and removed his mask. It was Zeno.

"Your guards?" he asked. "I have sent them away. They are under my supervision, as you perhaps know. You see I am able to do you a favor even yet."

"I suppose we must thank you," said Isabel. "If that act, however, is to lead to a repetition of the other night's folly, I must ask that our guards be returned to us."

"Never fear," he replied bitterly. "I have been that sort of a fool long enough and I have been well flouted for my pains. I am through. I have finally revolted against Topeltzin. For the last time I have been his deluded tool. Why, that scene I had with you the other night was for the absurd purpose of trying to make Zaliza jealous! For more than a year Topeltzin had held me in leash through promises of her love, and they have made a jest of me, both of them. I had my eyes opened last night, but too late. I had already done you a damage that I wish I could undo. The only atonement that I can make is to confess it to you and let you repair it as much as possible. I overheard your conversation in the garden and started to report all your plans to Topeltzin. I went only so far as the fact that Izon and Black Eagle were to make another attempt to escape, when Zaliza came to the door and Topeltzin stepped into the corridor to talk to her. I listened unseen and from what I heard them both say I have determined to join forces with Topeltzin's enemies. You will not be hampered with your guards to-night. Good-bye."

He limped quickly away. The girls were left speechless. It was Mariam who first regained her composure and faced their problem.

"We must get word to the men as soon as we possibly can," she said. She was studying Isabel's costume as she spoke, and a sudden idea occurred to her. "These garments no doubt were sent to us by order of Topeltzin, for we found them in our apartments, marked for us," she said. "It might confuse his plans somewhat if we assumed a new disguise."

They returned at once to their apartments, but in Mariam's plan they were doomed to disappointment.

THE MASKED FESTIVAL

Every outer gown of any sort had been removed from both suites since they had last been dressed, and none of their attendants were in sight. They looked at each other in dismay.

"Never mind," said Isabel. "We will do the best that is left to us."

"But whatever we are to do let us do quickly," rejoined Mariam, and at once they donned delicate masks of mica, which, while effectually concealing their countenances, enabled them to see perfectly. Then, with quaking hearts, they sallied forth into the palace grounds.

CHAPTER XXIII
FRIENDS IN THE DARK

THE two girls had scarcely entered the garden when they were accosted by a swaying pair of revellers with hideous bird-like masks. Thoroughly frightened, they ran; a course which would have been absurd except for the befuddled condition of the pursuers, who found themselves unable to thread their way amid the crowd and at the same time keep track of their quarry. Those against whom the girls jostled, being fully occupied with their own diversions, and accustomed to unexpected jolts and bumps, paid but little attention to them. Notwithstanding this the fugitives grew more terrified with every step, and they were immeasurably delighted when, at the side of one of the grottos, Isabel's eyes discovered a little clump of bushes behind which was a dark space where they might crouch. Slipping unobserved into this haven, where they could have a full sight of every one that passed them on one of the main paths, close enough

FRIENDS IN THE DARK

almost to touch the swinging garments, they remained concealed for some time. They caught frequent glimpses of Izon and Black Eagle, but saw to their dismay that they were allowed but to barely pass each other, never being permitted to remain in converse again. Evidently Topeltzin had given particular directions that they should not have any opportunity for concerted action.

Presently a Spanish cavalier, stalking stolidly along as if entirely indifferent to the two stalwart guards that followed close behind him, paused just in front of where the girls were concealed. Isabel immediately emerged from her hiding place. She had hoped to be able to attract his attention quietly, but he stood now with his back toward her, gazing moodily down over the gardens and out across the canyon itself. There was no way for it but to approach him boldly and this Isabel did, appearing to ignore the guards.

"Well, my cavalier, it seems that you have no time for Spanish girls," she chided him, a double allusion, intended to deceive the guards as to her identity and her costume, that of a Spanish maiden of the noble class.

The cavalier, still looking out over the canyon, suddenly swept his arm around her waist and swung her off her feet, at which the guards laughed. It was the first time that their taciturn charge had shown a disposition to take any of the license expected of every one that night. Isabel gave a laughing scream as she felt the strong arm sweep her up from the ground. She was a trifle surprised by the suddenness of the action, but not at all averse to it since she supposed it was Black Eagle who had thus grasped her. As she was caught up to him, another figure, which she instantly recognized as Zeno by his now familiar mask and limp, joined them and quickly whispered, so low as to be inaudible to the guards, "Go to the steps leading into the palace from this terrace, you and Mariam," then laughed aloud as the cavalier, throwing Isabel lightly over to his other arm as if she had been a feather, swung her back to the ground, still looking down over the gardens and across into the canyon, a proceeding that the guards and the passers-by hailed as a thoroughly good joke.

Isabel stood perplexed for an instant. Then she ran back to Mariam. What had happened? Was this a trick of Topeltzin's to inveigle them into some fresh danger? There was no time for her to decide. Every

FRIENDS IN THE DARK

minute was precious, and she resolved desperately to take the chance, to trust that it was aid rather than hinderance which was being offered her. Seizing Mariam's hand she hurried off in the direction of the steps. Just at the foot of the stone stairway stood a masker, looking savage enough in the ogrish disguise he wore. The girls stopped when they saw this uninviting figure. As they stood undecided he took a step toward them, holding out his hand, but seeing that they drew back in alarm stopped where he was. The girls might have been frightened had not their former tormentors of the bird masks once more appeared upon the scene. With exultant yells these new arrivals sprang for the cousins, but did not reach them. Like a flash the man at the base of the steps was out, and deftly tripped up these rowdies of the nobility and sent them sprawling upon the ground.

"Have no fear," said he; "I am Tepultac, at your service, and here comes Zeno. I have been waiting for some time. We are here to guard and protect you."

Isabel looked in surprise at Zeno. If there was not another trick here he was making good his promise to help their cause. Had Zeno been alone she would still have felt very much in doubt as to his intentions, but the presence of Tepultac, who also spoke to her, reassured her considerably. The men did not explain why they were there, however. They stood with the girls at the base of the steps for a few minutes, watching the crowd that danced by the path, but a few feet away from them, and ready for the defensive against the bird maskers, who, after a moment in silent menace, moved slowly away. No one was using the stairway, and behind it was a space of semi-darkness. Near to this space the quartet gradually drew, and Zeno, who was narrowly watching the crowd, suddenly said,

"Now step back quickly."

The girls did so unobserved. Underneath the steps they found another Spanish cavalier, sitting, concealed, upon a broad stone, where it was quite dark.

"Which one is Isabel?" he asked.

Isabel thrilled as she recognized Black Eagle, and she stepped forward, completely puzzled as to how he had preceded her to this place. He drew her quickly down beside him and pressed her to him.

"The last few minutes have seemed an age," he said.

FRIENDS IN THE DARK

"I had begun to think that I was doomed to sit here until morning or until I was discovered."

"Sit here?" she repeated. "Why, did n't I just see you out there by the parapet and did n't you amuse every one by tossing me around like a baby?"

Black Eagle chuckled. "It was not I and you would never guess who," he said. "It was our good Captain Helox. Zeno who, for some reason I don't see through, has suddenly turned our friend, got Helox out of the dungeon to-night and put him in a duplicate of my armor, leaving him here. He decoyed my guards and myself to this spot, and attracted their attention for the moment when Captain Helox was able to slip out from under here and take my place, thrusting me back. It was Zeno, too, who found a retreat in there for us to change our costumes — if Izon can ever escape from his guards. Of course it is impossible to duplicate the disguise he wears, or we would arrange to play the same trick for him that Captain Helox did for me."

When he had said "in there" he had nodded toward a little recess in the wall. It did not look as if any concealment could be possible in that apparently solid stonework, and Mariam, after looking at it with a quite natural curiosity, wondered about it. Black Eagle explained.

"There is another thing for which we owe Zeno our thanks," he said. "It is one of Topeltzin's secret chambers. That whole stone panel is centred vertically on a pivot, and swings at a touch when its catch is released."

A huge drum on the top of the palace tower struck the hour. Black Eagle arose impatiently.

"It is growing late," he exclaimed, "and we have done nothing. Our whole plan is likely to be balked if Izon's guards cannot be diverted from him. They have been unassailable so far. They have been plied with drinks which have had no effect upon them. Fights have been started in their vicinity to attract their attention, but all to no purpose."

"With very good reason, no doubt," rejoined Mariam. "It is quite likely that their lives are at stake."

"Let them die, then!" said Isabel, suddenly, rising to her feet.

She, usually accounted the "feather-brained" one of the pair, had suddenly become the thoughtful one, the

FRIENDS IN THE DARK

brilliant one, the daring one. She realized as keenly as did Black Eagle the desperate nature of the situation, and how every minute lost counted heavily against them in favor of their enemy, the high priest, and the imperative necessity of quickly separating Izon from his guards. She had evolved a plan which was worthy of Delilah herself, but it was one she could not explain to Black Eagle. There were certain features of it to which she knew he would most vigorously object, but she was not going to let this consideration stand in the way.

"Come, Mariam," she said, "we have escorts now, and I believe can brave this den of wild animals once more. Black Eagle, I think I can promise to send Prince Izon to you without guards in fifteen minutes. Wait until he comes."

She swiftly pressed his cheeks between the palms of her hands, and was gone. Accompanied by Zeno and Tepultac, the girls again mingled in the crowd and began looking for Izon. As they hurried through the gardens Isabel briefly explained her plan to Mariam, who was shocked by its recklessness, and she uttered a protest, but Isabel's reply was sharp and to the point.

PRINCE IZON

"This is no time to consider the proprieties," she said. "It is a matter of life and death, and you know whose life is most in jeopardy at this moment."

The answer was enough to silence any devoted woman. Pressing her lips together, Mariam assured Isabel by a clasp of the hand that she could be counted upon to play her part. All this time they were hurrying toward where they had distinguished Izon's costume in the centre of a gay group. The predominant vocal note of the revel now had risen to a shrill shriek. Servants were hurrying to and fro in every direction, bearing flagons of the strong wine which the Aztecs had brought to perfection. The group surrounding Izon was no less hilarious than the others. Izon alone among them was secretly oppressed. He was inwardly fuming that he could not for even a moment free himself of his surveillance, and was seriously considering the plan of strolling to the parapet and trying to fling his guards over. Moreover, he had not seen Mariam or Isabel all the evening, and he had hoped that long before this they would have been able to reveal themselves to him.

He was both shocked and surprised when they burst into the circle, laughing loudly and exchanging quick repartee with their two escorts. Their masks had been purposely allowed to slip so that they concealed but half their faces, and they could easily be recognized by any one who knew them. The nobles knew the girls well, though they had been given but little chance to cultivate them. Now they welcomed their advent with shouts, and Izon was pained to see that the girls apparently welcomed their advances. Mariam, to his intense surprise, seemed to be the freer of the two, and presently he noted that she was the centre of a little circle composed of nobles and his guards; that in raillery her wits were keener and more nimble than he had suspected it possible in her. He looked about for Isabel. She had suddenly disappeared. His guards were just behind him, seated at the stone bench at the side of the grotto, almost within touching distance of him and ready to spring to their feet at his slightest suspicious movement. Isabel was standing just in front of them now. As he turned she stepped backward and suddenly sank to the bench with a groan. The bench was not wide enough for three so perforce she fell upon the two guards.

"My ankle!" she gasped, and then sinking backwards as if fainting she threw her arm out as if for involuntary support. It fell about the neck of one of the guards, and her head was upon his shoulder while she was half supported upon the lap of the other one. Izon sprang toward her, but she raised her head as he bent over her, and, as if confused at finding herself in such a position, she quickly drew her arm away. She attempted to rise, but sank back weakly.

"No," she said to Izon as he stooped to assist her. "Do not bother. These gentlemen will attend me, I am sure."

Her mask had slipped off entirely now and she smiled sweetly at the half-intoxicated and susceptible soldiers as she waved Izon away. He caught her eyes and for a fleeting instant he read in them an expression of deep meaning. As if in corroboration of the thought that had come to him, Mariam at that moment rushed up to him, laughing.

"Protect me, Prince!" she cried. "These wicked fellows are about to cast lots for me," and, indeed, one of the nobles had spread his cloak upon the ground and was rattling some tiny golden dice in his hand.

Izon put both arms about her, and, looking over her

FRIENDS IN THE DARK

head, announced in a voice that echoed their own spirit of reckless fun as near as he could make it,

"You are too late, gentlemen. I have already gambled for the lady and won!"

CHAPTER XXIV
TLAX AND ZULM

THERE is one curious and startling fact connected with the downfall of every nation. In all times men of the highest rank and nobility have pursued women other than those to whom they owed allegiance and have consorted with them, and the nation has endured. But when the women of the nation, the mothers of the race, have done likewise, then that nation's last bulwark has given way and it has died. Rome was not overpowered from without until it was undermined from within by its Messalinas. When patrician ladies seduced by idleness and luxury have become morally frail, or when, wearied by the weaklings of their own effete class, they have turned to the lustier men of the lower orders and have become the pursuers instead of the pursued, that nation's doom has been sealed.

Such was the case in the Red City. It was merely Nature's own protest against the degeneracy which threatened there the extinction of human kind; it was

TLAX AND ZULM

Nature's own demand for readjustment, for new virility, and it told in characters as burning as the hand-writing on the wall that the long score of licentious pleasure had come now to an accounting.

Sheltered as Mariam and Isabel always had been they could not know this. They had only felt in some indefinable way that the women of the Aztec nobility were of abnormal seductiveness and beauty, and that the men were far too effeminately handsome to appeal to their own wholesomeness, and this was — had they but known it — another tell-tale symptom; for male beauty is ever weakening. Isabel, consequently, would have been shocked had she fully known how well she had succeeded in her appeal to the senses of these stalwart guards. They were of Topeltzin's picked soldiery, men low of brow, coarse of feature, brutal of mind, but perfect of body from the purely animal standpoint, and scarcely a day passed but admiring eyes gazed lingeringly upon them from out of oval, high-caste faces. They were, then, more nearly prepared than Isabel could have dreamed for this action of hers. They thought that they understood it perfectly and they exchanged significant glances.

PRINCE IZON

"I feel very faint," said Isabel in a low tone of voice, glancing up to see that for the moment Izon and Mariam had distracted all attention from her. "I shall have to ask you to help me to my apartments where I can have my ankle attended to and lie down a while." Involuntarily the two guards glanced at Izon. She understood the obstacle that lay in their way, but she had calculated upon and provided for all this. "Mariam," she called, "you and the prince must follow us. These gentlemen are going to take me to the palace."

She attempted to rise. The guards were immediately on their feet and lifted her up between them, the lusty boors thrilling already with the touch of the firm, rounded modelling beneath smoothly slipping silken fabrics. If she had but known, she need have done nothing more to have fed the embers that were glowing now in their eyes, but in her ignorance she fanned the flaring coals into devouring flame. She attempted to take a step or two supported by the brawny soldiers, but the effort apparently gave her intense pain.

"You will have to make a chair with your hands, I believe," she said, laughing lightly, and then showed them how to clasp their four hands upon their four

TLAX AND ZULM

wrists in the manner with which all children are familiar.

Isabel sank upon the improvised litter and passed her arms about the necks of the two barbarians, who, lifting her from the ground as though she had been a feather, found their jaws pressed against her shoulders. Stooped thus awkwardly, they started in the direction of the palace. Izon and Mariam followed and the nobles that had surrounded them would have joined the procession, laughing and joking and making a jest of it all, had not Zeno and Tepultac at that moment created a diversion. Had it been necessary they would have fought with each other to have attracted attention to themselves, but the two men of the bird masks sweeping up at that moment, arm in arm and singing at the top of their voices, Zeno and Tepultac immediately, one from each side, bumped them into each other. They were nearly knocked down by the force of the impact, and as they stood off to gaze at one another tipsily, the two meddlers shoved them again. This time they glared at each other, only half conscious that their uncomfortable predicament had been caused from the outside. Zeno slipped behind one of them, and pushing suddenly upon his elbow, thrust the fist smartly into the other's face. That was enough. The two instantly engaged in a ludicrous attempt to fight, and the crowd that might have followed the prince stayed now to enjoy this sport. Drunken, there was but small difference between the patricians in the gardens and the plebeians in the plaza.

In the meantime Isabel was being carried toward the palace and had her guards at a decided disadvantage. It was impossible for either one of them to look back handily, but to prevent them from becoming too uneasy she kept talking to Izon, and the even tones of his voice in reply put the guards more at their ease. When they reached the stone stairway Isabel turned to Izon.

"You and Mariam sit on that bench for a moment," she directed. "It is not necessary for you to come up with me. These gentlemen will be down again at once."

She had difficulty in keeping her voice from trembling, for this moment was the supreme test. Here was where she intended to separate from Izon. She could feel the guards pause simultaneously, then they came to a dead stop with their two foremost feet upon the same upward step. She could feel by the very tenseness of their poise that their duty and the consequence of any failure was burning deeply into their minds. It was a critical instant, and she gave a little gasp of dismay as she realized the further sacrifice that she must make. The cry of protest, almost a vocal one, welled up within her, but she stifled it sternly back. Her cloak, that had been draped loosely from her neck, she now slipped by a dexterous twist so that her shoulders were bared and at the same instant the faces of the men touched in turn, as they swayed, the flesh of her neck; their cheeks lay upon her silken skin. The contact was electric, and the quickened breath of her carriers told, to her dismay, how more than successful her ruse had been.

"Come," she said, "you must hurry and get back!"

Torn by conflicting elemental emotions, the men mounted the steps, and, though they had not forgotten Izon, nor Topeltzin's instructions, they consigned both duty and danger to oblivion. Isabel's heart was beating swiftly now. She realized at last that these were wild beasts whom it was not safe to unleash, but her task was not yet accomplished. It would be necessary to exert her abhorred wiles for at least ten or fifteen minutes until Izon and Black Eagle would have an opportunity to change their costumes, and once more she was compelled to set her woman's wits to work. She glanced back in deep concern in time to see Izon and Mariam, guarded by Zeno and Tepultac, slip unseen under the archway that screened Black Eagle. This much at least was accomplished, but by stretching back her head and turning she had heightened once more the effect that she dreaded, and her soul turned sick within her as the cheek of the fellow on her right hand pressed down upon her uncovered shoulder, while his chin pressed upon her bosom. She could feel the instant tightening in the tension of his arms, and the sense of it nearly choked her. She turned her head quickly, and, with a muscular movement of her shoulder, thrust his head aside, but even now she did not try to free herself, in spite of her wild impulse to spring from them and fly. One factor of safety remained to her, she suddenly reflected. There were two of them, and if she could but pit one against the other her entire problem would be solved.

They had now reached the top of the steps and were upon the terrace. To the right lay the entrance to the women's corridor, but it was not part of her plan to get inside.

"Air!" she gasped. "I must have air!" and this time there was no feigning, she felt the imperative need of it. "Set me down on the bench for a moment until I rest," she commanded.

Without any parley they obeyed her, carrying her swiftly to a bench in a shadowed angle. They put her down between them, and an arm of each sprang up at once to grasp her with an embrace of fire. She could have shrieked in terror, could have wept in her humiliation, but there is no one thing in all this world so marvellous as the fortitude and self-control of a woman that is put to the test. Stifling every impulse of agitation that would have betrayed her she played her next card and marvelled herself at the steadiness of her cajoling voice.

"Prince Izon," she reminded them. "One of you must keep an eye upon him."

The remark was well in keeping with their supposition of the case.

"Tlax may go," said the one upon her right, laughing gruffly.

"Zulm may go," retorted Tlax.

The devil that led Samson to his doom, that made a weakling of Mark Antony, that has been the death of a thousand kings and the life of a thousand wars, came in answer to Isabel's invocation for aid, and though she shrank from their touch as she would from the coil of a snake, she laid her warm palms upon the right hand of Tlax and upon the left hand of Zulm where they pressed upon her.

"One of you must go," she said, sinking her voice to just above a whisper. "The prince cannot be watched if you both remain with me, nor can I be quite — pleased!"

She hated herself for that beguiling tone, but not faltering, nerved herself courageously for a most desperate ordeal when she now suddenly arose. The two men immediately sprang up after her. Tlax made to clasp her about that rounded enticement which glowed alabaster white in the dim light, but Zulm interposed himself. For a moment, red-eyed, lower lips protruding, jaws set, nostrils distended, facial muscles working convulsively, shoulder muscles undulating, stocky legs planted firmly upon the stone-paved roof, the two bulldogs glared at each other through darkness and intense silence that were so fraught with pulsing passion that Isabel stood rooted to the spot, her heart thumping so loudly in her own ears that it drowned out even the sounds of revelry in the garden below, so loudly that for an instant she took it for the sound of measured, hurrying feet coming in an endless charge upon the stairway. Her knees trembled and in her limbs there was not enough strength to lift their own weight. Suddenly, with low growls like the involuntary warning of tigers that are about to spring, the two men clashed together like the thud of bodies fallen from a great height. They swayed silently but desperately, striving for a fatal throat clutch. They reeled and stumbled, legs and arms and bodies hooked in an inextricable embrace, and then suddenly they fell to the floor where they silently rolled, writhing and straining, each striving for that grip which would mean the settlement of all rivalry. They were the elemental males that, throwing all other consideration aside, battled out voicelessly and desperately their supremacy and fitness before the onlooking doe.

The shock of the fall gave to Isabel momentary strength enough to totter over to the bench and sink back upon it, battling desperately against the faintness that strove to blot out her consciousness.

CHAPTER XXV

TEZCATLIPOCA LISTENS

TOPELTZIN, smiling grimly, returned from his round of the gardens, where, inconspicuously masked, nothing had escaped him, not even the substitution of Captain Helox for Black Eagle, nor the ruse by which Prince Izon and Black Eagle were given an opportunity to exchange costumes. Helox he quickly detected and, with a smile that more resembled the snarl of a wolf, he planned a surprise for the doughty captain. Helox presently found himself being led toward the palace by his guards, and before he was certain that he was detected, he was suddenly hauled into an apartment, stripped of his costume, and turned into a luxurious room where a special banquet was provided for him. He shrank as he realized the hand of Topeltzin in this. Evidently some torture worse than death would follow, for he knew the diabolical ways of the high priest, who feasted well his especially marked victims before he wracked them soul and body.

TEZCATLIPOCA LISTENS

The high priest was mightily pleased with himself as he entered his favorite tower room, containing the golden image of Tezcatlipoca, and as now he found the shining figure confronting him, strangely luminous from the moonlight which, streaming in at the windows, fell directly upon it, he saluted it profoundly. "O Tezcatlipoca," he prayed, "Great God of Land and Sea, and above all and beyond all, Lord of Eternal Youth, to you I now appeal for that endless youth, by the fruits of the work I have done in your service."

Advancing to the window and pointing to the gardens and the plaza below he continued, still addressing the golden image.

"Behold, O Lord of Joyous Youth, the pandemonium I have created in your honor. This vast concourse I have assembled and set aflame to celebrate your feast to-morrow! They dance, they leap, they shout, these your subjects, they are engulfed in a mad riot of the senses which I have flooded upon them. They gorge, they swill, they brawl, they ravish, they kill — see, there goes one with a shriek, pitched over the parapet, to dash his carcass upon the rocks in the canyon below, to be swept away as so much wrack by the flood — all for you,

PRINCE IZON

dread Tezcatlipoca! True, it does not equal the services of my ancestors for you in the glorious days of Anahauac when twenty thousand quivering hearts were offered you on one day, but only consider, O Lord of Youth, the exalted rank of the victim to-morrow and it may outweigh even that gift!"

Raising his arms in the fervor of his supplication, and speaking in a low, tense voice, the high priest continued: "But now behold my finest gift to you, Lord of the Spring of Life — see me moulding these men and women so they will all contribute to the great sacrifice in your honor to-morrow — moulding them not by the force I could use, but by their own weakness and passions — surely, dread Lord of Youthful Emotions, nothing can be more pleasing to you than this? For lo! these men and women are now in the grasp of my hand and I have only to close that hand to crush. But why should I soil the hand? They have chosen to raise their puny wits against me, to combat me with guile, and with guile I shall lay them low; with guile I shall strike them at my feet to writhe in body, in mind, and in soul, each one unto his own special capacity. Can you, O Tezcatlipoca, desire more refined torment than this?

TEZCATLIPOCA LISTENS

"First Izon the proud, he that by his every look tells me daily that whatever may be his fate he will meet it proudly. I shall break that pride." His voice vibrated with passion. "Between two hells his choice shall lie, and to whichever one his anguished footsteps turn he shall find a shattering of all that he holds dear or sacred. He shall feel a humiliation from which the tortures of his body shall be a welcome relief; and, to heap more bitterness and agony upon his woe, he shall lose the love of Mariam and gain her contemptuous scorn, to which that spit-fire Zaliza shall add the final rankling scene.

"Scorn too, the scorn of Black Eagle shall be the portion of Isabel, and for the savagery that still underlies and animates his veneer of civilization, there shall be a special torment devised, and they shall all four hate and despise one another, this quartet of precious friends. As for the Spanish beauties themselves, Isabel, she of the raven hair, the Juno form and orbs of night, Mariam of the golden tresses and rose-tinted cheeks, they, when they have turned in loathing from their false lovers, shall not be without a haven. They shall find it — in this clasp," and grimly smiling he lifted up his mighty arms — in-curved as if already there lay within them the trembling prey that he had marked.

For a moment he mused in silence and then frowned.

"And these, O Lord of Youthful Joys, after all are but the trivialities of your coming triumph, for see, God of the Garnet Eyes, how I love you, and know it by the hatred I bear your enemies! Over there is your stupendous teocolli, your temple, O Tezcatlipoca, and pitted against it in the upper city is the fretted and chased and sculptured temple the Christians have raised to their deity. He is but a myth, a figment of the mind, a bogey to frighten and whip into submission the puling children that have no sentience. But there are those who believe in Him. It is they whom I must destroy, and in destroying, destroy their God; and one happy day I shall sink these talons deep into the vitals of Zolcoma who, just as I tell of your omnipotence, Lord of Pleasure, tells his unthinking sheep wonderful stories of *His* greatness and of *His* presence everywhere, and his sheep are like my sheep. They devour the foolery, not thinking even that in this crisis had *He* been so powerful *He* would long since have rescued these people who are now in my power, and especially this prince whose heart

TEZCATLIPOCA LISTENS

will soon be thrown, quivering, at your feet, O Tezcatlipoca."

Looking down upon the brilliant moving picture in the gardens below, Topeltzin's keen eye noted that a small army of servants was already serving the hundred banquet tables on the upper terraces of the garden, and he turned with sudden brusqueness away from the window. As he did so the moonlight suddenly increased in brightness and enveloped the image with a glow that caused its garnet eyes to sparkle until the entire golden figure seemed brilliant with life. Topeltzin, already wrought up by his own emotions, was transported by the sight and, falling on his knees, "Oh, Lord of Life," he cried, "now that the gage is thrown between you and the Christian God, give me, your champion, invincible powers that on the morrow *your* temple shall be the scene of *your* glorious triumph!"

Thrilling with the exaltation of demoniac fervor Topeltzin was startled by the image suddenly fading from his sight. A cloud had cut off the moonlight. Springing to his feet he reached out to the statue, but misjudging the distance, his heavy arm struck the image and it fell crashing to the tiled floor. Still in darkness

PRINCE IZON

he stooped, and finally grasping it, he replaced it on the pedestal just as the light came in, but to his shuddering horror he saw that the garnet eyes were shattered, the features crushed, its face in the pale moonlight now the simulacrum of ghastly death!

CHAPTER XXVI
PRINCE IZON — TRAITOR

THE two stalwart figures of the soldiers, terrifying in their vague outlines and stilled at last, lay over in the shadow where they would be found in the morning still and cold, with reddened knives clasped within nerveless fingers. They had cheated the punishment which Topeltzin would have inflicted upon them for their negligence. Isabel, so long as the uncannily noiseless struggle had endured, sat fascinated, the tensity of the drama being enacted before her eyes helping her to throw off the faintness that had come upon her; but now, some subtle instinct telling her that the curtain had fallen on this latest enactment of the world-old tragedy, she sprang in horror from the bench where she had crouched with every nerve astrain, and rushed to the balustrade near the top of the steps. It was like coming from a world of dim, dead shadows to the land of light and life. There, below in those gardens, while there might be wickedness, there were at least human eyes that sparkled and human lips that smiled, and, though the lower gardens were deserted now, since the vast company of nobles had thronged to the upper terraces where the alfresco banquet had been set, she rested her eyes eagerly upon them, drinking in the brilliant scene, breathing deep into her lungs the new breath of life, and regaining control of the faculties that she might yet be called upon to exercise that night.

She turned at the sound of approaching footsteps, and her heart gave a bound as she recognized the familiar armor of the Spanish cavalier. Could it be Captain Helox? She hoped that it was. If it was Black Eagle it would mean that they had been frustrated in their plan of changing costumes; if Prince Izon, that his escape had been cut off. Her uncertainty was quickly to be dispelled, for as the masker neared her he raised the visor of his helmet and she saw the countenance of Izon. He came quite close to the balustrade, where the light from the gardens below shone upon his face within the helmet.

"Prince!" she exclaimed. "Lower your visor quickly before you are recognized!" and reaching up she herself drew it down. "What are you doing here?"

she continued. "Could you not get through the gate as was planned?"

Her own mask had been removed and her face was upturned to him in anxiety.

"What am I doing here?" he answered her in a deep, earnest whisper. "I scarcely dare to tell you, but the time has come when I must. I know that I am taking a desperate chance at this moment when I am about to go away, possibly to be overtaken and killed, possibly to never see you again, but I must tell you the secret that devours me. Isabel, I love you, have always loved you, since the first day we met in the canyon! I feel that you, too, have known this and have helped me, like the brave woman that you are, to dissemble. Now that the last moment has come, however, we must keep up this mockery no longer," and suddenly clasping her in his arms he drew her to him in a passionate embrace.

Amazed and shocked, Isabel attempted to struggle, but was powerless in that resistless clasp which had pinioned her arms to her sides.

"I cannot understand you!" she exclaimed. "This must be madness; I cannot believe that it is treachery to Mariam!"

"Mariam?" he replied in apparent surprise. "Do you mean to say that you have not understood, that you have not seen how I loved you and was compelled to hide my real self; how I had to seem to be attached to Mariam so that I could throw her to Topeltzin as the price of my liberty?"

Isabel gasped. The tone was earnest and convincing, and she felt all her hold upon a belief in humankind swaying and giving way. The events of the night had piled upon her with one crushing weight after another, but this was the heaviest, the most unbelievable, the most intolerable of all.

"Mariam!" he repeated, his voice aquiver with whispered vehemence. "Poor child! She is good, it is true, and pretty in a way, and there are those who doubtless greatly admire her style of beauty; but she is a waxen figure, a painted sculpture, a statue of tinted ice, while you — you! — Why, in that other city to which, if I am spared, I shall spirit you away, I shall make you queen! And I shall dare to possess that which I have always coveted, the most exquisite being that the sun has ever shone its ardor upon, or that the night has ever hidden away beneath its shadowy mantle to feast upon in the darkness! Ah, Isabel, you are a figure that a sculptor might despairingly strive a lifetime to carve or a painter to depict; you of the scarlet lips, you of the raven hair, you of the glorious eyes of fire, Isabel I *love* you!" And once more he tightened his embrace about her, pressing her head closely upon his shoulder, crushing her resistance as if it were a yielding filament spun in the morning dew.

"Infamous!" gasped Isabel. "Prince, you leave me no course but to believe you, and it is infamous — *infamous!* If it were not for the awful peril that surrounds us all I would cry out and deliver you to your enemies. Let me loose, and go!" and bursting into tears of rage and shame, she again struggled impotently in his arms.

"I will not take that as an answer," the fervid whisper replied. "You do not know what you are saying. When you realize the depth of the love that I have been forced to conceal, its intensity, its glorious pain, and its bitter joy; when you recall the veiled words and the burning looks I have given you from time to time as chance offered; when you are over the surprise of the secret that I have told you, I know that your heart will turn to me as mine has always turned to you. Why, think! How could you imagine that I could see you so often without yielding to the spell of your fascinating charms; your face so exquisitely lovely, your form so surpassing beautiful, your eyes so melting, so dreamily soft, so seductively overpowering! How could I feel the thrill of your magnetic look, and not be so enchanted that my very soul longs to melt with yours in ecstatic bliss?"

Isabel looked about her wildly for aid. It seemed to her that this night was marked for every humiliation that could be called down upon pure womanhood. Anger and sorrow struggled within her for the mastery over her abasement.

"Oh, Prince!" she cried. "I have lost more than my own happiness, my own self-esteem, my own faith in mankind — I have lost a brother. In his dear stead I have found a traitor, faithless to Mariam, to Black Eagle, to me, and to you yourself. Go! For Mariam's sake I will give you time to get away if you can. Hurry, lest anger conquer my grief. Will you let me go or shall I call?"

"Good-bye, Isabel," came the whispered answer, and,

PRINCE IZON—TRAITOR

once more pressing her convulsively to him he let her go. She staggered back a pace and covered her eyes, the tears trickling through her fingers. He turned from her toward the open garden, for a moment lifting his visor again as though to let the cool air blow upon his heated face, and as he stood there with the light from the gardens gleaming upon him and revealing the pale, set countenance of Prince Izon, he saw, rooted stock still and flanked by guards, the tall figure of Black Eagle in the resplendent costume that the prince had worn at the beginning of the evening. Black Eagle, stunned, stricken, motionless, was staring straight at him, and had been during the whole scene upon the terrace. The visor was hastily dropped, and with a shrug of his shoulder, its wearer disappeared in the opening at the side of the tower.

Isabel had not seen Black Eagle. She had no thought for him nor for any one else at that moment, for her brain was in a whirl. The blows that had been dealt at her self-respect one after the other were almost more than she could bear, and she sat upon the balustrade to weep, forgetful even of those two awful forms that lay over there in the darkness, clasped in death's embrace.

Black Eagle, however, the moment he saw that now hated figure in armor disappear from the edge of the balcony, aroused himself from his stupor, comprehending at last, with all that was savage in him coursing back from a hundred generations, and gathering force and momentum and virulence until it burst upon his heart in a fury that caught him up and shook and wrenched him until his very soul writhed in agony. His civilization was cracked and shattered into fragments, and in an instant he had been turned by his jealousy into a raging demon. His brain reeled, bright corruscations flashed before his reddening eyes, his fingers twitched convulsively. Suddenly he sprang forward. The guards were upon him in an instant, one gripped to either arm, but with a frenzied wrench of his mighty body he flung them off as if they had been but yelping curs, and with a snarling, half-articulate imprecation that left flecks of red-tinted foam upon his drawn lips, he dashed toward the palace. His breath came in spasmodic gasps from the very depths of his lungs, and rushed hot and searing from his mouth with a succession of wheezes like the laboring of a wind-broken horse. He gasped out raging cursings in an unknown jargon. Back from those generations of blood-glutting savages whose virus coursed now so riotously through his veins, had come snatches of the crude mother tongue. He was a devil, a living, leaping, devastating tongue of the fire of vengeance and for him there was no Red or Pearl City, no paganism or Christianity, no sacrifice or rescue, no Topeltzin; but, written gigantic across the whole scope of his heavens and his earth, there was but the one blood-red thought of revenge!

Mariam, slipping up in the shadows from the lower gardens, barely missed him, but had she met him face to face he would not have known her. Only one vision filled his retina, a picture that would not fade and that crowded out all other sight, the memory of Izon there upon the terrace clasping *his* Isabel passionately in his arms. Mariam quickly gained the roof terrace. Isabel arose at the sound of her rapid footsteps upon the stairway and hastily dried her eyes. She was trying to think what she should say to soften the blow that she must deliver to Mariam, yet she had had no chance to formulate it for Mariam rushed up to her and embraced her joyously.

"Good news, my dear, brave girl!" she said. "He

P R I N C E   I Z O N
is safely away, thanks to your ruse, and even now is hastening towards the wall, guided and guarded by our good friends Zeno and Tepultac. He left me in the corner of the lower garden a few minutes ago," and once more she embraced Isabel and kissed her warmly.

Isabel stepped back startled and gazed at Mariam almost in terror.

"What is that you say?" she faltered. "Whom did you leave but a few minutes ago?"

"Why, Prince Izon!"

CHAPTER XXVII
UNMASKED

ISABEL gazed upon Mariam with distending eyes and growing dread. There was some hideous misunderstanding here, some mystery that she could not fathom.

"Impossible!" she gasped. "You say that you left Izon a few minutes ago?"

"Yes."

"And that you actually saw his face?"

"Saw it! Why, plainly, and more than that —" and here Mariam's cheeks flushed warmly, "I — I felt it!"

Isabel's brain was all adaze. She almost had doubts as to her own sanity. It was impossible that Izon should have been in two places at once, but, according to Mariam's account, he must have left both of them at practically the same moment, and must have spent the previous minutes with both of them simultaneously. Again and again she had Mariam assure her that she could not possibly have been mistaken, until Mariam herself was alarmed for Isabel's mental condition, and smoothing her hair gently away from her brow as one might soothe away the disordered fancies of a child, inquired anxiously into the cause of her perturbation.

"Mariam," said Isabel solemnly, "there is some great danger encompassing us, something more dreadful than anything that has threatened us yet. I do not know what to think or what to do. I am frightened more than I can express. It is uncanny, unbelievable. Suppose that I were to tell you that Izon left me but just a moment before you came, that he had been with me for several minutes before that, that he was holding me in his arms against my will, that he was making the most violent love to me!"

It was Mariam's turn to gasp and then she laughed nervously.

"It isn't a good joke at all, dear," she replied. "You might have scared me if it had not happened that I can still almost feel the warm clasp of Izon's arm about me." Isabel attempted to smile in reply, but it was a very wan smile and Mariam, smoothing her hair gently, went on. "I cannot think where you got this strange

UNMASKED

idea, Isabel. I know Izon. I would know him in any disguise, even had he not raised his visor for a good-bye kiss, and I am very, very sure that I could not be mistaken about that. Now, could I?"

Isabel shuddered.

"No, of course you could not," she assented, trembling. "But, Mariam, here is the terror of it. I could not be mistaken, either. I swear to you that it has been only a few minutes since he came up to me in his armor, here, where we are standing now; that at the very beginning of our talk he raised his visor and I saw his face clearly in this bright light; that as I live he made the most violent love to me, almost smothering me in his arms, and when I upbraided him for his treachery to you he swore that it was I whom he had loved from the very first!"

Mariam turned pale and faint. She had been studying Isabel intently and she was satisfied now that it was not madness which possessed her cousin, and the same dread which had shaken Isabel sent its chill tremor over her.

"Could it be possible that there were two Izons?" she queried in half-whispered awe. "Can it be that there are really such things as wraiths, or as demons that take upon themselves the forms of living men to their undoing? I have heard of such things and have looked upon them but as foolish, ignorant tales; but in such a case as this what can one believe? Of only one thing I am sure. If there are two Izons, it was the right one who spoke to me in all loving truth. There is nothing, Isabel, that could make me doubt him; I cannot imagine who talked to you. But be he man or devil, it was not my prince!"

Even in the midst of her tormenting doubts Isabel thrilled with pride in Mariam's steadfast faith.

"What can it mean?" she asked in fright. "I, too, am quite sure that it was no wraith that held me, and now I shall fear the shadow of every leaf. There is evil in the very air, I think, evils past and present and evils still to come. Even while we are wondering upon this present mystery we are forgetting another tragedy that affects me still more nearly. What has become of Black Eagle, or what will become of him? It must be close now to the hour of unmasking, and if Black Eagle is still in the costume of Prince Izon, then there is a fair chance that the prince has escaped."

U N M A S K E D

In palace and gardens, tinkling bells scattered about the grounds, upon the towers, and within the long halls, set up their silvery harmony. It was the signal for the state banquet, when would be found the solution of their anxieties.

The minor nobles had been feasted in the garden, but those of higher titles, most of whom had held aloof from the more boisterous though equally licentious revelling, were now to be feasted in the banquet hall where the ceremony of unmasking was to take place, and where great Tezcatlipoca himself, in the person of Prince Izon, was to preside. These bells were the signal for the assemblage, and the girls, impatient now to know the fate of Izon and Black Eagle, hurried into the palace and up to the corridor which opened upon many latticed balconies, overlooking the banquet hall. Here they could see though they could not be seen.

No Oriental splendor could compare with the gorgeous luxury spread out before them. The walls and ceiling of the large hall were tapestried with feather work, so delicate that it looked like superb porcelain inlay, though without its cold glare. Dominating all the designs were blazing golden suns, one at the top of

PRINCE IZON

each panel, while from just below a great red human heart dropped its crimson beads across the ivory field. Borders to these panels were of representations of the sacred quetzal bird, each tiny design picked out in its natural colors and each in itself a work of art which had taken weeks of patient labor to accomplish. From the vaulted ceiling there depended chandeliers of hammered gold, each of which bore a cluster of lights. Upon the floor were arranged couches for the three hundred banqueters, who reclined upon them while being served. One end of the hall was screened off by an intricate golden lattice behind which sat the ladies of the higher nobility — for in these solemn state functions no women could take part — while at the other end of the apartment was an elevated dais for the prince, Topeltzin, and other dignitaries. There were flowers everywhere, the same crimson blossoms that had been in such significant evidence for the past two days; they flamed in rare bowls of hollowed crystal, the couches were strewn with them, they filled, in flowing masses, urns that stood upon quartz pedestals at the intersection of each row of couches, and the very floor itself was thickly carpeted with them, their faint, sweet odor perfuming the air.

UNMASKED

The hall was unoccupied now, except for a solid row of beautiful female slaves around the four walls, clad in soft draperies that outlined the perfect symmetry for which they had been chosen. They stood motionless, tense, elbow to elbow, their hair parted in the centre and waving at either side over the brows, to be caught up with a diadem at the back and then streaming down between their shoulders. They formed a living dado around the entire hall, and had been so thoroughly trained that there was not even the swaying of the single figure, the uneven shifting of feet, the wavering of steady, bright, forward-directed eyes. It was a strange and wonderful decorative effect wrought in living flesh and blood by the consummate master-artist, Topeltzin.

Now strains of music issuing from some hidden recess added their intoxication to the languor of the perfume, and with the first notes the head of the glittering procession of masked nobles entered the hall through the gold-studded portals at the side. Two by two they marched slowly in, brave in their pomp of rich raiment. In two lines they separated to the two sides of the hall, a vivid and brilliant concourse of fantastic costumes, gleaming in every bright color and rich with the sheen of feather work that had cost the eyesight of many a toiler. Here were gems that in the markets of the world would have been worth the ransom of kings, and here were golden ornaments that, aside from their marvellous workmanship, would merely for their weight alone, have represented a fortune in any spot outside this El Doradic canyon.

There came a clash of music as the last of the nobles came in and arranged themselves silently upon their couches and there followed a brief space of tense silence after the last of them had disposed himself in comfort. The living dado still held silently, motionlessly to its place, while a hush, more tense than the mere silence itself, fell upon the assemblage. Now it could be seen that a square of couches in the centre of the hall and adjoining the dais at the end, was still empty. Once more the music began, but now it was a stately chant in which, however, there was an undercurrent of something intangible, indefinably menacing, something that rang, somehow, of diabolical cruelty; and now there entered another procession, gray-robed, gray-cowled, gray throughout except for relieving edges of crimson, and

UNMASKED

except for a blazing sun with a red heart in its centre upon the breast of each robe. Here was the real nobility of the Red City's empire; here the real rulership, this powerful gray band of the priesthood that cast its sombre shadow over every life, that held within its grasp the destinies of every being within the confines of the Red City, from the proudest noble to the meanest slave. It was an autocracy, invincible, inscrutable, that moved in the dark and exhibited only its results to the light.

Once more the music ceased, and again that tense, vibrant silence ensued as the last of the priests took their places, filling the vacant couches. A huge drum boomed out its strident announcement, quivering upon the silence like the forerunner of some impending doom, even though it called to gaiety. Twelve slow strokes it gave, and then the portieres behind the dais were drawn back, revealing a colossal golden figure of Tezcatlipoca much like that in Topeltzin's niche but here towering to the ceiling, its huge red eyes gleaming sombrely upon the waiting concourse. From the archway between its knees emerged Topeltzin and his council of a score, and then, last of all, after these had taken their places, standing beside their couches, came a litter carried by eight slaves

PRINCE IZON

and bearing aloft a tall masked figure in the gorgeous costume that Prince Izon had worn at the beginning of the evening. The litter stopped at the side of the throne-couch in the centre. Slaves helped the glittering figure down, and for a moment he stood before his throne. Again a stroke of the drum boomed out its summons. Topeltzin raised his hand and removed his mask. It was the signal for unmasking, and the girls in the balcony, who had been standing with their arms clasped about each other, now drew tightly together in dread of the next moment when, Black Eagle having unmasked, the rage of Topeltzin would know no bounds, and they looked to see Isabel's lover turned over to hideous torture, perhaps before their eyes.

There was a rustle of the hundreds of masks as they were removed, then the hand of the towering figure by the throne went up to its head and removed the golden, quetzal-crowned casque, revealing to the triumphantly smiling Topeltzin, to the nobles and priests, to the women behind the lattice, and to the two cowering agonized girls in the balcony, the face of Prince Izon!

CHAPTER XXVIII
THE BETRAYAL

THE unmasking of Izon, signal of unutterable dismay to Isabel and Mariam, was also the signal for the beginning of the feast. Suddenly, leaving the four walls, the living dado melted into fluttering units, turned from a waxen decoration to a quickly moving flock of houris, each one assigned to a separate banqueter. Theirs it was to lift crystal goblets to thick lips, to convey delicate morsels to coarse mouths, to press perfumed napkins gently upon hanging chops, to support drooping heads upon rounded arms, to bear upon occasion the weight of shoulders upon soft breasts, to take away all necessity for exertion, and to render free from all distraction the refined gluttony which at this day attended the high perfection of the gastronomic art in the Red City. It was to these hand-maids that the flagons of rich wine were passed, to whom all food was first handed that they might serve it to these loutish lords of creation, who, grown fat of their voluptuous living, had become mere flaccid, breathing automatons of sensuality.

Soft music once more mingled with the perfume of the flowers, and course after course of rich food succeeded each other, but these details were lost upon the girls in the balcony. How had their house of cards, erected with such infinite pains and at such distressing sacrifices, come to be destroyed, to fall clattering to the ground? There was no answer. It was only another overwhelming mystery added to the many dark enigmas of the evening. Suddenly heavy footsteps sounded outside in the corridor, and in a moment more Black Eagle stood before them. His attire was dishevelled and his face was convulsed with anguish, while his eyes were blood-shot and there was a moisture upon his quivering lips as he sank upon his knees before Mariam and wrung his hands, shaken and unmanned.

"God help me, Mariam!" he cried. "I dare not ask for your pardon, but only for your pity. I have destroyed my friend!" and his huge frame trembled with emotion.

Mariam, herself terrified by his appearance and action, even beyond the quaking terror that had already

THE BETRAYAL

laid its cold clutch upon her very heart, faltered for words.

"Tell us at once, good friend," she cried, "for we can bear no more suspense. We are heart-broken and crushed, and we cannot understand."

"Nor can I!" cried Black Eagle. "Least of all can I understand how I could be a traitor. Yes, both fool and traitor!"

Isabel, from whose eyes the tears were now streaming, could not speak, but she reached forward and laid her hand upon his head in great love and pity. The touch seemed to goad him into fury, and he struck her hand aside as if it had been a poisonous snake.

"It may be fitting," he cried in blazing scorn, "that traitor should fondle traitor, but I will not. I have too heavy a load to carry even now without adding to it the degradation of *your* wanton touch! Isabel, let me tell you that while all I hold most dear is shattered past all hope of healing, I shall live even under that burden; live, if for no other reason, that I may remember your name to hate it, remember your face to spit upon it!"

Isabel had borne up to this moment all and more than ordinary women could have withstood. Her

PRINCE IZON

dreadful experience with the two guards, their fight to death, the unwelcome love-making of Izon, the startling mystery that was unfolded with the coming of Mariam, the shock of the unmasking when Izon was revealed in the place of Black Eagle, all this she had endured, though her heart had been disordered by the succession of shocks until with the least exertion it beat tumultuously within her bosom and with the least quietness it died down to only a feeble fluttering. But now, with this sharp dashing away of her hand, and this furious renunciation of her, the limit of her strength was passed, and, groping upward with her fluttering hands as if she would place them upon her bursting head, she swayed and fell.

Some time before she could open her eyes her sense returned and she knew that she was reclining upon a bench in the balcony, and that Mariam was gently fanning her while talking to Black Eagle.

"You have misjudged her," Mariam was saying. "We are all the victims of some terrible plot that I am sure is due to that diabolical Topeltzin. I know that you saw her apparently in the arms of Izon, but that she did not resist his advances, I know is *not* true, for

THE BETRAYAL

she told me the whole story as soon as I came to her. Whatever else has happened I would swear to Isabel's loyalty, in spite even of the evidence of my own eyes. Her heart is yours and yours alone, as it has always been."

"I would have staked my life upon it until to-night, just as I would have sworn to the fidelity of Prince Izon," answered Black Eagle, with still a trace of the anger that possessed him, although he was trying his best to control it. "Alas for me, Mariam, in Izon there was no fault. Oh, my wretched blunder that fills me more with woe, if such a thing is possible, than the disloyalty of Isabel, for with my own act I gave the innocent Izon back into the clutches of this monster who will rend him. I have told you how I saw Izon and Isabel in that fervid parting upon the roof terrace; I have told you how I rushed to the palace, but I could not describe to you, so that you would understand it, the paroxysm of hate that possessed me. I rushed to the hidden stairway back of the tower, where I imagined Izon must emerge, but evidently I had gotten there too late, for he was gone. Next I rushed back to the guardroom and blurted out my news to Gautemotzin that

PRINCE IZON

Prince Izon and I had changed disguises and that the prince had escaped, and with that the work was done. They lay in wait for him at the lower gate where I told them he would go. Within five minutes they had located him. The two that were with him escaped unidentified. The guards paid no attention to them, for it took all their forces to capture Izon alone, since it must be accomplished under pain of death if they blemished or even bruised him.

"It was before the evil Gautemotzin that they brought him, after they had taken Izon's delicate robes from me, and that ugly demon of Topeltzin leaned back in his chair and laughed like a very devil! I could have throttled him for that laugh, and I would have done it, I think, but for the great fury that shook me when Izon, whom I then thought so false, stood before me. I made a spring for the prince. I remember a half-articulate roar of anger that burst from me as I plunged toward him, and found my grip fastened upon the throat of one of the guards that had interposed. I was so blind in my rage that I did not know the difference. I strangled and shook him like a rat until the other guards tore me back, raving and stained from my own blood that had sprung from my mouth and nostrils! It was Gautemotzin who had them pour over me vessels of cold water until the blood had receded from my brain, else I should have died then and there, I know, in the very torture of my passion. When I had somewhat come to myself, the calm, reproachful voice of Izon addressed me.

"'Black Eagle, my more than brother,' he said sorrowfully, 'what has come upon you?'

"At this I raved again, but the desire to upbraid and execrate him, to tell him of his perfidy, helped to give me coherence and I poured out upon him reproach after reproach. But when I had almost exhausted myself with my bitter tirade, I coupled his name with that of Isabel and charged him that I had seen him embracing her upon the roof terrace, confirming the suspicions I had once before entertained. I could not escape from his look of shocked surprise, though I charged him even then with being a most consummate actor. He denied that he had seen or spoken to Isabel since he had gone into the chamber under the stairway to change costumes with myself, but the denial only fanned the flames of my wrath anew.

PRINCE IZON

"'Lie!' screamed I. 'Lie upon treachery and treachery still upon lie! Listen, then!' I shrieked, shaking my quivering finger at him, 'and remember this when you lie on the stone and the obsidian knife hovers over your shrinking body! Remember that it was I who betrayed you, that it was I who brought you back, that it was I who sent you to the sacrifice!'

"No answering rage met mine. In the eyes of the noble prince there was nothing but sorrow and pity.

"'Comrade,' he said, mournfully, 'comrade and friend still — unless some devil has misled you — why have you done this thing?'

"'Through jealousy,' said a mocking voice, and to my amazement another figure in armor joined us and raised his visor, and then I thought I was surely demented, for another Izon stood before us. 'Guards,' said the second Izon, as he closed his visor, 'once more these gentlemen may exchange their costumes. You, prince, shall again don your triumphal robes and shall preside at the feast as was originally planned, under pain of the instant death of your women guests as the penalty for aiding you to escape. In the olden days of Anahauac such a noble representative of Tezcatlipoca

THE BETRAYAL

as the prince would have been subjected to the ritual of merely physical tortures, preliminary to the sacrifice, but they were coarse tortures, affecting only the body. In these latter days we are more refined; we prefer to work upon the mind. You can revel in the knowledge that Mariam believes that you have embraced Isabel and repudiated herself. Now for you, my fine friend,' addressing me, 'you have shared in the attempt to escape, thus interfering with us, and as a reward for this you have had the pleasure of seeing Isabel in the loving embraces of a mail-clad man whom you supposed was Izon, and, acting upon this belief you have betrayed your friend who was entirely innocent. How do you like betrayal and treachery, you who have boasted of your loyalty to the death? Moreover, you now may guess whom it was that shared those loving embraces with your entirely willing sweetheart. I am going to tell you, and I wish you joy of your present emotions. It was myself — the other Izon — at your service!' and upon this he raised his visor and took off a waxen mask of the face of Izon fitted within the small face opening of the helmet — displaying to my astonished eyes the satanically smiling features of Topeltzin!"

CHAPTER XXIX

TEMPTATION

THE confession of Black Eagle was broken by the voice of Isabel. Her returning consciousness, quickened by what Black Eagle had said, revived with new strength.

"So it was from the mouth of that fiend," she said, pointing an accusing finger at Black Eagle, "that you heard the accusation that I willingly accepted his embraces — and you really believed it? After he had shown you the infamous lie he could construct, you actually chose to believe him, to add to my distress the burden of your savage jealousy?"

Black Eagle stood aghast at the charge. His emotions had been in such riot that he had no place for logic. Believing Isabel guilty after what he had seen, he had not been able, in the swift course of exciting events, to divest himself of that impression. Before he could say anything, Mariam, too, turned upon him.

"The first thing Isabel told me when she met me,"

TEMPTATION

she sternly informed him, "was how the man she supposed to be Prince Izon had held her gripped in his arms with such power that she could not even give evidence of struggle, that she had protested and had bitterly upbraided him for his perfidy to me. Was not that enough sorrow, barbarian? Come, Isabel," and rising, Mariam helped her cousin to her feet and together they started to leave the balcony.

A sob, a man's dry sob, stopped them and they turned back. Black Eagle, abject in his abasement, was upon his knees, and now he caught the hem of Isabel's robe and pressed it to his lips. For a moment Isabel looked down upon him, trying still to be stern, and then she suddenly threw herself to the floor beside him, and, taking his head in her arms, pillowed it upon her shoulder, soothing him as a mother might a wayward but forgiven child. With the choking sobs that shook him she mingled her own tears, and in that moment, for the first time, was full and perfect confidence established between these two stormy souls. Never again could jealous suspicion come between them.

Calmer moments succeeded, and Mariam, who had turned back, found them sitting upon the bench, Isabel nestling confidingly in Black Eagle's arm. She sat down by them, and now once more, gravely and seriously, they went over their situation, particularly as it affected Izon. As they compared notes and discussed the matter in its various phases it gradually dawned upon them how many-sided and how far-reaching was the plot Topeltzin had concocted. Izon would think now that Mariam and Isabel would both believe in his perfidy, naturally supposing that Isabel would tell Mariam what had transpired on the roof terrace. Thus he was laboring under the intolerable misery of thinking he had the scorn of both the cousins and that his best friend had betrayed him! For a few moments they were silent, appalled by the diabolical skill of the high priest, each wondering where it would strike next. Suddenly, a new thought came to Isabel.

"How did you get here?" she asked. "You left off your story when you and Izon were both in Topeltzin's hands."

"Simple enough," he explained. "When Topeltzin gave his ultimatum that Izon must continue the banquet programme on pain of your death, of course he could only consent. While this was going on, Tepultac had

TEMPTATION

slipped into the room and was one of the most vociferous of the priests in denouncing me for aiding Izon. Completely deceived, Topeltzin ordered him to take charge of me under two guards to be led to the dungeons. As we passed the steps to this corridor, Tepultac curtly dismissed the guards, telling them that he would himself fasten my dungeon door, and then left me to join you here, to tell my miserable story! And that reminds me that I must now go to meet Tepultac," he continued. "We must get news, through Azra, to the Pearl City to-night," and with a hearty hand-clasp from Mariam and an embrace for Isabel, he left the girls alone.

They remained there watching the course of the banquet. Stimulated by the rich wines they were drinking in enormous quantities the feasters were becoming loquacious, and loud talk and laughter resounded throughout the hall.

The select party on the dais where Izon was the centre was no exception to the general hilarity, and if it were possible, the admiration of Mariam and Isabel for Izon was intensified by noting that he was not showing the slightest apparent trace of disappointment or chagrin. Quite the contrary, he was sustaining the dignity

PRINCE IZON

of his position just as he had done ever since his entry into the Red City, with perfect ease and grace.

Topeltzin was the chagrined one. He was obtaining none of his anticipated satisfaction, but on the contrary was forced secretly to envy and marvel at the superb appearance and bearing of his rival.

The admiration of Izon which, as Zeno had reported, had spread over all Ixtol, now culminated among these banqueters in a real appreciation of his matchless courage, by repeated and sincere toasts and cheers, until the royal banquet hall resounded with the mighty acclaims. All the instincts of a glorious line of ancestors were aroused in them at the sight of this debonair young prince, in his magnificent costume and noble attitude looking the veritable god he represented, and the great ovation to him was no mockery but came spontaneously from the hearts of all; excepting, it need hardly be said, from Topeltzin.

At last the drum, concealed behind the statue of Tezcatlipoca, sounded out its summons. Slowly and with difficulty the over-stuffed and wine-drenched nobles and priests rolled and tottered to their feet, and, leaning upon the girl slaves, staggered into the formation of a

TEMPTATION

wavering double line and passed from the hall. Swift, noiseless slaves cleared the dais of all its tables and couches except the one upon which Izon reclined. The lights were extinguished, excepting the soft glow of tinted lamps upon the dais, which lay now in a soft, artificial twilight that quivered with the incense of a circle of censers, hanging from the circular dome above. The music changed once more to a sensuous, rhythmic strain, and now the curtains that screened the archway between the knees of the giant Tezcatlipoca, swayed and opened.

Garlanded with flowers and clad in filmy draperies that gave swaying lines of motion without concealing aught of rounded perfection, a troup of young girls, picked daughters of the highest nobles, selected for their grace and beauty and flawless symmetry, whirled in, and, surrounding Izon's couch, raised their sweet, fresh voices in a choral song to which their gently undulated bodies kept perfect time as they slowly circled about him.

> "Life is short and joys are fleeting,
> Rapturous hours are thine to-night;
> Drain the cup of Pleasure's nectar,
> While our charms drive care in flight.

PRINCE IZON

> Night o'er all descending darkly,
>   Bids Love's revels hold full sway;
> Youth and beauty cling together,
>   Clasping dalliance while we may.
> Onward dancing, joys entrancing
>   Smile upon you where you lie;
> To thee stealing, senses reeling,
>   Bend thy slaves with longing sigh."

The chant ended, the music changed slightly, an increased tempo and a raised pitch of the same strain giving it a curious rhythmical abandon, and then began a sinuous, alluring dance, such as the breathless girls in the balcony would never have imagined could be devised. In it was all the seductiveness, all the witchery, all the enticement possible to exquisite, ivory-tinted limbs and supple rounded bodies, and it had its base in the very wellsprings of all humanity, of all breathing, sentient life — the appeal to quickened senses, which animates all dances of whatever variety. Here, however, aided by shaded lights and soft music, by languorous perfume and luscious wine, the appeal arose to an insistence well nigh irresistible as the graceful figures swayed and undulated, pirouetted and curved, swelling busts and rounded limbs appearing in ever new and more enticing conformations as the figurates themselves fell under the

TEMPTATION

sway of their own ardor. For these were no mere hired, or even commanded, ballerinas; they were the pick of all the regal beauty that the Red City boasted, and they had been drilled in the postures of this enkindling ceremony by that master of all the sensuous arts, Topeltzin, since the first week after Izon's capture. Now, the great event had come, and they were earnest and eager in what they did; for, perhaps, Prince Izon might, by simply the raising of a hand, choose one or more from among them — an honor past all reckoning by the standards of Aztec teaching ingrained in their heredity for countless generations.

Thus inspired, no gesture was without its yearning, no glance was without its flaming invitation, and if the senses of Prince Izon reeled — why, the provocation was nigh irresistible. The circle now contracted as the music took on a more insistent timbre; it grew smaller and smaller until the dancers, still circling slowly and still more slowly, passed him, rounded bosoms heaving their seductiveness enhanced by jewelled hands partly screening the charms which the drooping gauze exposed as they bent low before him, curved scarlet lips half-parted, white teeth gleaming, delicate nostrils distending, rounded cheeks flushing, half-veiled eyes smouldering and glowing and burning!

If it was an ordeal of fire, Prince Izon gave no present sign that its flames had scorched him, for he let them circle completely around him in this last supreme effort to arouse him to a choice; then, smiling, he waved them away and they receded to the dying cadences of music, crestfallen but kindled for the dissolute orgy to follow with the priests. Izon drained at a draught the huge flagon of wine that was brought him by a dwarf, the latter selected, because of his hideousness, to throw into sharp contrast the entrancing loveliness past and to come.

There came another phase of the music, tremulous, low, gliding, inexpressibly sweet, and suddenly a single figure stood before the prince. She was an exquisite creature, one of the three chosen for the supreme honors in this ceremonial. Jewels sparkled in profusion from her lustrous hair, on her hands and arms, and even upon her delicate ankles where the laces of her tiny golden sandals crossed; they glittered, too, like spangles upon the gauze that clung to her superb figure, and with every move that she made they flashed and gleamed and shot

TEMPTATION

forth rays of scintillating color. She danced slowly and with infinite grace, keeping time to the wreathing weft of her gyrations with softly clicking castanets, now advancing, now retreating, now circulating so near to the couch that the web-like hem of her perfumed garment brushed the prince, now winding out of reach as if to leave him utterly.

"I am sick, Isabel, sick and faint!" cried Mariam, and buried her face upon Isabel's shoulder. "Take me away! I can look no more!"

Isabel soothed her for a while, pondering upon their situation but becoming more and more angry as she thought of the devilish ingenuity of Topeltzin.

"Poor Mariam," she said presently, "but poor Izon, too. I also dread to stay, lest I see him make a choice."

"Impossible!" cried Mariam, starting up and looking at Isabel with terror-stricken eyes. "Impossible! You forget our love, my cousin."

"I forget nothing. In the first place, Izon is a man, and so, human. He would scarcely be one that you could love if he were less, or more; for you, my Mariam, have the life of love within your own veins. In the second place, Izon thinks that you must, at this very moment, despise and scorn him — thank that demon Topeltzin for this one more refined cruelty. In the third place, the wine may have been drugged for Izon all evening. In the fourth place, by the laws as Topeltzin has revised them, if Izon accepts his wives he is given some space of time to live a life of luxury with them, and in that time he may still embrace Tezcatlipoca and live, or even escape, but if, on the other hand, he refuses them, he goes to the sacrifice at once, and can neither help himself — nor us. Shall you blame him, if Izon, being a man and therefore, as I said, being human, if he — "

"Don't," cried Mariam, and put her hand over Isabel's mouth. "I cannot stand it."

But Isabel had a sudden startling idea of her own, and persisted in the torture.

"See," she exclaimed, "that girl has gone! The prince has waved her away — for the time — at least — and once more is unscathed. But Mariam! He gazes after her and sighs. He is sitting bolt upright now, and he drinks the wine that is offered him as if his tongue were parched and his throat burning. Look, Mariam, look!"

TEMPTATION

"I will not look," cried Mariam. "I cannot look!"

Once more she hid her face, just as the music burst forth into a more sensuous strain. For a moment Isabel bent forward, surprised, incredulous, angry. A new dancer had appeared within the illuminated space and had whirled into the mazes of the measure with an abandon that was electric.

"Mariam, I think that you will look now," Isabel said grimly. "This is something that you will want to see, that you *must* see, and then, I will tell you of a plan to save your love, if it is not too late. Look, Mariam! You must look!" and lifting her cousin's head with her hands she turned the pale face around toward the dais.

Mariam gave one glance, and then a half-coherent cry sprang to her lips while her hands clutched at her bosom.

The second dancer was Zaliza!

CHAPTER XXX
THE THIRD CANDIDATE

IT was not the first intimation the girls had been given of Zaliza's infatuation for Izon, infatuation that had dated from his first triumphal entry upon the palace plaza, and, understanding her impetuous nature, they could readily anticipate the witchery and passion that she would weave into her dance. And it *was* thrilling, the tingle of it seemed to pervade the very atmosphere, to mount even up to that far-distant balcony and appall the watchers there with its potent pulsation. Here was no mere invitation, here was compulsion. Like a lambent flame she leaped and quivered, a wild thing of living beauty, the very embodiment of devouring desire. She advanced in open-armed, startling rushes, she retreated in coy affectation; she encircled him like a whirlwind, she drooped gracefully before him as if to swoon and be caught within his arms, and all the while she never missed perfect step and the time in the most bewildering dance that he had ever beheld.

"Isabel!" sobbed Mariam, "it is true, all true that

THE THIRD CANDIDATE

you have told me! My poor Izon! See, the wine is in his blood, his eyes are glowing, he follows her every movement! I am going to call out to him — to remind him of our love — to tell him that I am here!"

Isabel grasped her arm as she sprang to the lattice.

"Don't!" she cried. "You can not make him understand or even hear. Come with me. I have a better plan."

"Where are we going?" asked Mariam breathlessly, as Isabel dragged her by the wrist through the balcony corridor.

"To the robing room," replied Isabel, still dragging her cousin onward. "I am going to costume you, and you are to be the third candidate."

Mariam stopped, jerking her wrist from the vigorous clasp, and stood, her face crimson, looking at Isabel with wide, incredulous eyes.

"You don't mean that!" she gasped. "Why — "

"But I do," insisted Isabel. "Hurry. We have no time to lose."

"But — but — why, it is impossible!" stammered Mariam. "I could never appear in such a way, especially before Izon. I should die of shame."

"You will die of a worse shame if you do not," retorted Isabel, angrily. "Look at that, and see if it is not your turn to make some sacrifice!"

They were just passing another balcony opening, and Mariam, looking out, felt the flame of jealous anger flash up in her cheeks. Nothing was real now, but this. So much of the unusual and unnatural had transpired here that the entire night seemed one long, fantastic nightmare, in which no incident was so startling that it did not become commonplace in the next event.

"Come," Mariam said simply, and herself led the way. Burned now into her consciousness was the knowledge that she would rather see Izon upon the teocolli than in the arms of this woman. A life is a thing that one must one time lose anyhow, nor know regret that it is gone, but a love that is lost leaves behind it a bitter pang that corrodes and anguishes while it does not destroy. And Mariam, bewildered and confused, believed that Isabel's plan, startling though it seemed, was the only way to keep that precious love intact.

They hastened down the stairway which led to the robing room, where the third girl was already being

THE THIRD CANDIDATE

prepared. Fortunately, she was already repentant of her bargain and dreading the time when she must appear — not that modesty thrust its blushing denial upon her, but that she realized the futility of trying to outvie that electrifying effort of Zaliza's, and she was one of those who sulk if they cannot excel. She was secretly pleased, therefore, to yield her place to Mariam, and assisted Isabel in the toilet with many an exclamation of wonder at the pure white loveliness of Mariam. Crimsoning until she was an exquisite mingling of pink and pearl Mariam stood while Isabel put the gauze robe upon her and clasped a stoled cestus about her, and then, when she was through, the cruelty of it all moved Isabel to compassion and she kissed her reverently upon the forehead.

"You are an angel, dear, as pure as the Lady Godiva herself, whom all the world has loved and revered since she, too, cast aside her raiment in a stern cause," said Isabel soberly. "And see, I will clothe you in the Lady Godiva's priceless robe."

Deftly she let down the golden hair which rippled in a shining cascade almost to Mariam's feet, and the Aztec girl who had given up her place could not keep from rubbing her hand over its silken strands, nor, having touched it, could she forbear from kissing it. A gasp of astonishment from one of the maids caused them to turn to the curtained archway through which they could see out upon the dais. Zaliza had reached the limit of her audacity. Whirling now in dizzying circles, the collar of gems about her beautiful throat scintillating and flashing like a ring of fire, she was extinguishing one light after another in the outer circle, after each extinguishment curveting in and away from Izon with tantalizing blandishments, stooping perhaps for a fleeting instant before him, poised with arms outstretched with all the light grace of a bird, bending over him suddenly, as if to take him up in her arms, advancing as if to throw herself in romping abandon upon him, approaching at another time slowly and coyly as if she half feared and half wished that he might suddenly reach out and detain her, now grasping the flagon of wine to bend it from his lips and touch it to her own, looking over the brim meanwhile with melting eyes gazing deep into his — Satan himself, much less Topeltzin, could not have devised a more potent, irresistible appeal to a

THE THIRD CANDIDATE

young man in whose veins ran red blood, who felt himself lost to love, who was plied with spiced wine, steeped in languorous perfume, beguiled with seductive music, and who could gain present immunity, perhaps life, by the mere yielding to these soft, twining arms.

The outer circle of lights had been put out, leaving only the inner circle of pendant candelabra which cast down but a dim halo about the couch where Izon, half-sitting and half-reclining, resting against the prop of one tense arm with his hand grasping the edge of the cushion beneath him, followed the incarnate temptress with half-smiling lips and eyes that smouldered. Suddenly Zaliza, with consummate art, trusting wisely to her further powers when Izon should be conducted to the luxurious apartments where the further and final tests awaited him, caught herself in the very midst of a dainty poise and like a humming-bird that is frightened, darted suddenly away, and vanished before he had even time to comprehend what she was about. He turned quickly to look after her, his gaze lingering in fascination upon the swaying curtains where she had disappeared. The hideous dwarf handed him a flagon fresh filled, but Izon took it mechanically, and, his gaze having been averted from the curtains, sat looking upon the rug at his feet, thinking, thinking — how?

Man is not responsible for all the thoughts that enter his mind, but only for those that remain by permit of his sovereign will. Izon's soul had expanded in nobility as he grew to manhood until, nurtured by his life of right living, it was as near perfection as man's can be. But now almost overwhelmed was he by the surges of poignant emotions by which he was deluged. The strong wines, the sensuous music, the seductive invitations extended by the lovely dancers breathing passion and desire, were nearly floating him into the realms of pleasure when "the still small voice," direct link between humanity and Divinity, now shielded him from the siren darts of their burning glances! But Satan had other arrows in his quiver. He now shot his most insidious one and as the thought penetrated Izon's mind, "What use? — despised by Mariam — betrayed by my brother — to die now means a disgraced oblivion; while by living, I can undeceive her and perhaps escape," — the voice of conscience was almost stifled.

Hovering now between heaven and hell was that

THE THIRD CANDIDATE

soul when the music resumed its endless song of love, and Izon became conscious that a new figure had glided into the halo of light, and he looked up slowly. For a moment incredulity and amazement possessed him in turns, and then, humbled yet glorified by the wave of feeling which swept over him, he realized that this great love which was his, was as far different from the spurious rapture that had been offered to him as the pure appeal of Mariam herself was different from the impure appeal of those others; for theirs was to the senses alone, while hers was to the heart, the mind, the soul, to everything that was best and truest within him, to all the gentle chivalry and nobler manhood that his wholesome nature contained.

Mariam stood before him motionless, slender, erect, dazzling white as compared with the mellower tints of the Aztec maidens. Even her face had lost every vestige of its color in this crisis of the supreme test.

Since she had taken the desperate and as it now seemed, to her timid self-consciousness, the ill-advised step that might possibly retain her hold upon the love of this prince among men, but might estrange it, she could only think to pray, and with her hands clasped and her

PRINCE IZON

eyes involuntarily upturned she was like a flawless statue of Purity, hewn from the sparkling white marble of Carrara.

Into the heart of Izon there stole an understanding of this strange and wonderful miracle of love that knew no bound and asked for no reward but love, and it humbled him. He loved her now, the heart and soul and brave spirit of her, as he had never loved her before. From her there radiated an atmosphere of sweet innocence, withal so exquisitely modest and ineffably chaste that he arose from his couch with bowed head. He approached her reverently, and sinking upon his knees, touched his lips to the pale hand that came trembling out to meet him.

With flushed face, eyes sparkling with rage, and heaving bosom, Zaliza stood peering at Izon from behind the portieres through which she had darted. For years before she had seen Izon, she had heard of him as the god-like ruler of the Pearl City, knew the tales that were related of his superb comeliness. All this had excited in her an intense desire to see and meet him, for she had found that the man did not live in her own city

Mariam before Izon

THE THIRD CANDIDATE

who could cast an indifferent look upon herself. When the news of his coming spread through Ixtol her strongest expectations were aroused and when she first saw him and found these expectations more than realized, her attempt to remove Mariam and Isabel, in whose beauty she saw rivalry, by exciting the mob against them, was the result of her hitherto unfettered wilfulness.

In the succeeding period this infatuation had been kept alive by the frank courtesy and admiration with which Izon had always treated her, by the occasional deeper glance which she fancied she had caught from his eyes, glances which no man had hitherto been able to veil in her presence. But beyond all this it was nourished by the hope that in the final scene when she would offer herself to him, if accepted, she could carry out a daring yet simple plan she had conceived for his escape with her to the Pearl City. In this, the final hour, she had thrown into her dance all this repressed passion of weeks and her whole being had thrilled with the voluptuousness of her emotions roused by her dancing in such close proximity to him. She felt, too, that his own emotions had responded to hers. She had noted as she bent over him, the answering flash of his eyes and as she had left him at the moment when, overcome by the intoxication of the dance she was apparently about to sink into his arms, she expected him to follow her into the inner room. As he did not appear at once she had tiptoed back to the portieres, and as she looked into the banquet hall she could scarcely believe her eyes for she saw the exquisite figure of Mariam standing before the prince. She could not fathom the mystery of it all, but when Izon knelt before Mariam the fury of the woman scorned flamed its maddening course through her brain.

She quickly made her way to the small banqueting room, where Topeltzin was presiding over the final orgies of the priests and the dancing girls. On low couches the priests reclined in company with the dancers, each of whom, feeling herself worthy to have been chosen by Izon, was consoling herself with the lesser honor; for honor this was deemed in the strange and contradictory ethics of these people.

Some were dancing around the couches the voluptuous dance of the Orient mingled with the swaying activity of the lithe Indian, a combination of sensuous enticement that swept into a blaze the senses of the priests, already inflamed by the spiced wine which they were still drinking in vast quantities. The beautiful forms of many of the dancers were wholly displayed, these having cast aside even the filmy draperies in which they had first appeared, and they wreathed in and out around the couches in entrancing undulations that ended only with their sinking into the arms of their lovers in ecstasies of voluptuous languor.

For a few moments Zaliza surveyed the scene with dilating nostrils yet scornful eyes. For a moment its mad abandon, so in harmony with her own feelings, impelled her to participate where she would be queen. But there were fibres of refinement in her being that the promiscuousness of it all repelled and the next instant the anguish of the loss of her triumph assailed her and with an imperious gesture she beckoned Topeltzin to join her in the corridor.

The high priest, although deep in the pleasures of the saturnalia, had imbibed but little, and quickly joined her.

"Izon has rejected your candidates, myself included," she said in a voice so tense with rage that Topeltzin could scarcely recognize it.

"What?" he answered. "I supposed by this time he would have had you in his arms."

"No! No!" she screamed, stamping her foot. "He has Mariam in his arms — he has rejected me and defied you."

Izon and Mariam had scarcely exchanged some hasty explanations when a band of guards burst into the hall. The prince instantly threw his cloak around Mariam, covering her from throat to feet, and turned to face — Topeltzin!

Rage burned and consumed the high priest so that at first he could scarcely speak coherently. His face was purple with anger and his clenched fists quivered. He had never dreamed of such a termination as this to all his carefully laid plans. It had been his intention to have turned Mariam against Izon, and Isabel, in reprisal, against Black Eagle, hoping with the mean and futile calculation of a man who knows nothing of purity to turn them thus to himself.

"Seize him and take him away!" he shouted hoarsely. "He has already made his choice, and to-morrow he dies!"

A number of guards rushed upon the dais from both

THE THIRD CANDIDATE

sides. The struggle was brief, for, borne down by weight of numbers, Izon was soon securely bound and dragged away. The shriek of Mariam followed him, and Isabel, fearing for her, rushed out to take her in her arms.

Topeltzin came close up to them, and, with folded arms, gazed at them with a sneering smile.

"Well, my gentle ladies," he mocked them, "tell me now who is the lord of life and death in the Red City?"

"You are, my lord," faltered Mariam. "Be merciful."

"I must be paid for mercy," answered Topeltzin with a harsh laugh. "Every commodity under sway of Ixtol has its price, you know. Isabel, you may leave us alone for a moment. I would have a word with this — this unexpected candidate."

"I have no secrets from my cousin," replied Mariam apprehensively.

Topeltzin smiled sardonically.

"Very well, then, she may remain, for, after all, what I have to say perhaps concerns you both. It is about this same Izon. Even he has the sum of his ransom fixed. Would you know, Mistress Mariam, the cost at which he may be set in secret outside the city walls?"

Mariam, studying his evil face, turned sick as she divined what that ransom must be, but still she must ask. She would leave no chance to slip by her without at least an inquiry.

"And what is the cost?"

"Yourself!"

"I thought as much," she replied steadily. "My lord, it is far better to die nobly than to live ignobly, and I have no hesitation in speaking the death warrant of both Prince Izon and myself. Yes, and I do it proudly, as he would have me do. We can both die."

"And by Great Tezcat, you shall die!" roared Topeltzin, the rage which he had been repressing breaking out in all its fury. "Take them to the red prison at once! If I cannot make you mine by consent, I will own you by force!" Suddenly remembering the onlookers, he sunk his voice to a sibilant whisper, "and then when tired of you, I will throw you to my soldiers, to be passed from one to the other until like broken toys

THE THIRD CANDIDATE

you shall be trampled under their feet bruised and crushed! And that shall be your death!"

Stamping with rage, he thrust his convulsed face close to the girls. As they shrank back, the robe which Izon had thrown about Mariam slipped from her grasp, and although Isabel quickly restored it, for the moment the lovely girl was revealed to the high priest. He stood petrified! As the eyes are dazzled when emerging from darkness into sunlight, so was Topeltzin's dark soul paralyzed by this vision of purity. Involuntarily he threw his hand before his eyes; but only for a moment and the reaction of evil came with redoubled force, thrilling him with his overwhelming, approaching triumphs. As the guards hurried the girls away, "Gods," he gasped, "what prizes — no wonder Izon resisted the others! — and now they are mine! mine!"

CHAPTER XXXI
THE LAST TEMPTATION

IZON in his prison room paced restlessly to and fro. His rank as Prince of the Aztecs and as titular divinity, which title he would hold until the sacrifice, had prevented Topeltzin, as he had wished, from sending his captive to one of the cave dungeons which had their noisome depths in the cliffs under the palace. Instead, the prince was confined in a large room having one window overlooking the river, making escape impossible in that direction, while outside the single door stood two sentinels. An hour had passed since Topeltzin himself had closed the door and Izon had heard his stern injunction of vigilance to the guards. In that hour the dire threat of the high priest "to whichever hell his anguished footsteps shall turn, he will find a shattering of all he holds dear and sacred" had almost proven true; for the captive prince could feel no hope.

He had reviewed the past; his calm and uneventfully happy life in the Pearl City; his numerous works of

THE LAST TEMPTATION

civic improvement and wise government; his longing for a mate that would be his for himself alone and not for his rank; his excursion into the outer canyon and the meeting with the hapless Mariam and Isabel; his recognition of his deathless love for Mariam; the fight in the canyon where some of his life-long friends had fallen in his defence; the alternative presented to him of death for the survivors or their lives and his assumption of the role of the visiting god; of the plans and hopes of escape; the weeks of joy in the society of Mariam and the winning of her love; then the catastrophe of this night when betrayed by Black Eagle — all his plans had been shattered, his friends perhaps killed, and himself an inevitable victim of the sacrifice in the morning.

As these thoughts came surging through his mind, Izon clenched his hands and ceased his restless walking. He had unconsciously stopped before the window and now his gaze wandered out into the moonlit scene of river and cliffs and pyramids extending in the distance. Its wondrous beauty recalled the banquet hall and the scenes through which he had just passed.

As a treacherous foe, when beaten in the day, will

attack his conqueror at night after he has laid aside his armor, so does temptation assail its victims in their moments of relaxation.

"What use," it whispered to the prince, "has been your rejection of Zaliza? Your friends have been confined and if not already killed, are helpless, and you are doomed." And the vision of the Aztec beauty as she bent over him in all the intoxicating fervor of her passion mocked him with the tantalizing pangs of a lost opportunity.

A slight creaking noise caused him to turn and as he did so, the door opened and a figure muffled head to feet in a priestly cowl and gown entered. Advancing, the robe was thrown aside and Zaliza in all the splendor of the charms revealed by her dancing costume, stood before him.

When Topeltzin had rushed in on Izon and Mariam, he had been followed by Zaliza who had witnessed the entire scene. As she saw Izon seized and dragged away she had exulted with all the cruel abandon of a gratified vengeance. But when she saw the calm dignity of Mariam, devoting both her lover and herself to death rather than accept life with dishonor, a mysterious yet power-

THE LAST TEMPTATION

ful change of feeling possessed the heart of this girl who in spite of her faults caused by her sinister environment was a noble and heroic nature. As she noted the reverential way the prince knelt to Mariam before taking her in his arms, as she realized at last the perfect beauty of her rival, the noble fortitude displayed by Mariam inspired her to emulate the Spanish girl in her devotion to Izon, and to let nothing stand in the way of proving her own greater love.

Thus it was that as she faced the prince in his prison her expression was very different from that which he had last seen in the dance; then all was the passionate fervor of invitation; now, her eyes were starry with unshed tears; her face downcast; her heaving bosom partly concealed by her crossed arms.

"Prince Izon," she said in a low tone, "I have come to aid you to escape; put on this cloak and hurry to the wicket in the garden wall. The door will be open for you."

"But how — ?" began the amazed Izon.

"The guards have been bribed," she interrupted him. "Go at once, before these sentinels are changed."

Now Izon was not slow to act but the events of the

night, the treachery of even his best friend, and the seeming omniscience possessed by Topeltzin, had rendered him suspicious. Particularly was this true of Zaliza on account of his rejection of her invitation in the dance.

"But, Zaliza," he asked, "who could have bribed these guards? Black Eagle, Mariam, and Isabel have no gold; my Luxtol friends could not have penetrated here to-night; — explain."

Zaliza hesitated. It was not her plan to let the prince know of her part in this affair until they were safe, and then he should learn it from others. She saw, however, by Izon's look that he would brook no concealment.

"O Prince!" she said, "understanding Topeltzin as I do, I know that having thwarted all your plans his vigilance would relax and few guards would be left on duty. These I have bribed, but only on condition that they accompany you to Luxtol to escape the vengeance of the high priest."

Knowing the wealth of Zaliza's family Izon could now understand, but he did not know and could not have wrung from Zaliza the fact that it had required all the

THE LAST TEMPTATION

jewels and gold of her inheritance to accomplish her end. As it was, however, Izon was deeply touched and as she stood and pleaded before him, the eyes of the half-distraught prince devoured her superb form, her flushed face and sparkling eyes. Never had Zaliza looked so lovely. Her physical charms were now rendered overpoweringly seductive by her loving earnestness and Izon felt their potency to the utmost fibre of his being.

"And you, Zaliza?" he asked.

For a moment she was silent and then with lowered eyes and head she answered,

"My lord, where could I hope for life and safety but with you in Luxtol? You know what the vengeance of Topeltzin will mean."

Izon swiftly considered the difference between this suggestion and the one tendered him at the banquet. The latter meant a temporary dalliance leaving himself and his friends still in Topeltzin's power, while now his escape to his own city was offered and the only objection to it was the obligation to Zaliza. As though reading his thoughts Zaliza spoke.

"O Prince," she cried, extending her beautiful bare

arms to him. "Come, let us go to freedom where in your own Luxtol you can gloriously reign on the throne of your forefathers!"

Izon stood gazing straight before him with the look of one viewing a startling sight. The walls of the room had disappeared and he beheld the summit of the teocolli; saw himself stretched and held on the sacrificial stone; felt the lengthened agony of the knife with which Topeltzin was prolonging his torture; saw his body cast over the parapet, hurtling and crashing down to be seized and later devoured by his captors of the canyon. Then the vision changed to the banqueting hall, where, emerging from the shadow of the background and illuminated brighter than the reality, the radiant vision of Mariam in the purity of her lofty passion swept over and enchanted his soul as the draught of a divine elixir, and so fortified his spirit that the thought of death or the depths of hell itself had no terrors for him.

Only a fraction of a second had elapsed and as the walls of his prison room again closed around him, he looked with pity mingled with gratitude upon the pleading Aztec beauty.

"Zaliza," he said gently, "deeply do I feel all that

THE LAST TEMPTATION

you have done for me, but it is impossible — I cannot desert my friends. If you care to help me further, go and comfort and if possible rescue them."

"O Prince," she wailed, "once in your own city at the head of your troops you can rescue them and meet Topeltzin on equal terms."

"No! you will meet him now on his own terms," said a harsh voice, and with horror and dismay on Zaliza's part and the hopeless conviction that all was lost on Izon's, the two saw the high priest standing in the doorway, and heard the sounds of a fierce struggle in the corridor succeeded by an ominous silence. Suspicious of even his most trusted guards since the Thlax and Zulm affair, Topeltzin had come in time to hear Zaliza's appeal.

"So, my rejected candidate," he said with a triumphant smile, as the leader of the guards entered the doorway and saluted him with a significant gesture, "only an hour ago you came to me to expose your friend here — which resulted in his involuntary retirement to this room — while now I find you about to lead him away."

For an instant Izon thought of rushing upon him

and ending the matter then and there but the faint hope that his friends might have escaped and that their plans for the morning on the teocolli might be carried out, restrained him, and he remained silent, surveying his foe with the calm haughtiness which was so galling to Topeltzin.

Zaliza was in despair. Her plan, so costly and venturesome, had seemed so near of fulfilment that its collapse almost crushed her. But this despair drove her to the last loophole of escape, the greatest bribe; the supreme sacrifice.

"O master of us all," she cried, throwing herself on her knees before Topeltzin, "do not punish the prince for my deeds. You surely know that he had no part in this attempt," then clasping his knees she whispered, "You offered Mariam on certain conditions to set him outside the gates — make me the same offer and perhaps my answer may be different from hers."

Topeltzin was staggered. Like all voluptuaries, who regard every woman with a single view, he had long secretly coveted this wayward beauty but, repulsed by her cool indifference, he was true to his axiom that there would be no pleasure in forcing her, and had taken

THE LAST TEMPTATION

pride in the thought that he had concealed his desire. But Zaliza had long penetrated his thought and now felt sure of her ground. For a moment the high priest hesitated, but only for a moment, as he recalled the glory of his approaching triumph and the further consideration that he could subjugate Zaliza at his leisure in the future.

"What!" he said to both, " deprive the good people of Ixtol of the feast for which they have been waiting so long? Deprive Tezcatlipoca of his victim's burning heart? The gods forbid! As for you," he said to Zaliza, "I regret to have to imitate the prince's rejection of you in so short a time, but your charms have been so freely offered to-night that they have lost their attractiveness."

Zaliza sprang to her feet. Medusa's face never looked more awful than hers. She knew Topeltzin's thought, — all hope was gone.

"O you fiend," she cried, her voice thrilling with concentrated rage, "you think you have triumphed, but just as you reach forth your hand to grasp victory it shall be snatched from you. There is either a Christian hell or an Aztec perdition and to whichever is the deepest and most horrible and everlasting, you are trying to send me; but if I go it will not be alone — to that perdition we will go together." Snatching a dagger which she carried she sprang at Topeltzin. Izon started forward but Topeltzin was quicker. He seized her wrist and throwing his free arm around her, instantly bent her hand so that the dagger pointed to her own heart and with a force that snapped the bone of her arm thrust the blade into her breast, where it remained as her arm fell limply. Instantly Izon sprang forward and, snatching the dagger, thrust at Topeltzin; but a guard seized his arm and after a fierce struggle in which the high priest warned his minions not to injure the prince's person, he was disarmed.

With a convulsive shudder and stifled cry Zaliza would have sunk to the floor but Topeltzin supported her, and now he pushed her over to the horrified and panting Izon. "Take her, Prince," he cried, with a diabolical grin, "take her now and while watching her, you will get a foretaste of how the sacrificial knife will feel as I thrust it slowly into your breast and twist it around when we meet in the morning on the teocolli!"

THE LAST TEMPTATION

And with a devilish leer he folded his arms and glared at his victims.

Izon supported the dying Zaliza and gazed with infinite pity and sorrow at the beautiful girl whose sparkling jewels seemed to mock her eyes now fast glazing in death. As he gently lowered her to a couch the drooping eyelids fluttered, then raised, as she tried to look into his face. Her breath came in shorter and feebler gasps as she whispered, "Izon — for love of you —," until with a last sigh and an attempt to smile and to open her eyes which finally closed like a tired child's, she faintly murmured, "In your arms — happy — at last — Izon."

The sounds caused by Topeltzin striding from the room, by the closing door, by the muffled groans of the bribed sentries as they were dragged away to the torture, by the treading of their successors in the corridor were not heard by Izon. He was alone with the beautiful dead.

CHAPTER XXXII

THE RED ROOM

WITH all the physical shrinking but inspired spiritual courage that animated the Christian martyrs as they were marched through dark passages to the arena where wild beasts awaited them, Mariam and Isabel were conducted, after the former had robed, to a strange quarter of the palace.

It was a room with walls, ceiling, and all furnishings of dull red. The color was so uniform that it was difficult to distinguish the outlines of such furniture as there was, but this color scheme was not its sole peculiarity; there were no visible openings of any sort, and when the guards, two fellows whose brawny shoulders sloped out almost directly from under their jaws, had entered with them and had shut the heavy pivoted door, its place could scarcely be seen. The light was of course artificial, but it too was tinted red so that the expression even of the two gentle girls were rendered almost saturnine, while the faces of the guards seemed diabolical.

THE RED ROOM

They sat calmly down, paying no attention to the girls, who, cowed and frightened, huddled up against the wall in agonized suspense.

This was broken by the voice of Topeltzin. He stood before them, but how he had entered they did not know.

"When I told you," he said with grim ferocity, "that you would be mine, I should have added that your lovers would offer no obstacles to our pleasures. Your friend," addressing the cowering Mariam, "will enjoy his last moments under my manipulations on the teocolli in the morning and there will be no haste — he shall have ample time to enjoy the penalty of opposing me; if you listen closely you will hear his screams of joy. As for your champion," he continued, shaking his finger, trembling with rage, at Isabel, "he is now having a foretaste of the hell where he is to go, and I have brought you both here to witness his transports of joy — "

His voice was drowned by the sound of hurrying clanking footsteps outside the room; by thick inarticulate roars of anguished rage which seemed to come like the bellowings of a maddened bull; there followed the sounds of heavy blows, each succeeded by that anguished cry — then silence. Topeltzin stood, hands clenched, eyes blazing, listening. Suddenly the hearts of the girls were almost stilled by a long-drawn, appalling scream of a being in the extremity of mortal agony.

"Now!" hissed Topeltzin, "look at your brave Indian! See how he enjoys his bed of roses!" Grasping the girls, he pushed them to the side of the room nearest the sounds. "Look!" as a small red curtain slid aside revealing a window filled with a mica sheet through which the horrified girls could see into the next room, "See your lover stretched on a fiery gridiron — see his limbs being twisted — see the burning pincers — hear his screams!" He ceased, further words being wasted, his captives having sunken in a huddled heap to the floor.

Topeltzin motioned to them contemptuously with his foot. "When they recover and send for me," he said to the guards, "you will find me in my lower room," and he strode from the apartment.

The sound of his footsteps had scarcely ceased in the corridor when the outbreak in the torture chamber was redoubled, causing the girls to revive and stagger

THE RED ROOM

to their feet, seeing in the dim light the victim engaged in a furious fight with his tormentors. They reeled against the door to the red room which burst open, and the struggling mass came tumbling in. Even in the dim light the hideous mutilations could be seen on the blood-covered face and body and only one fierce eye remained to glare out upon his tormentors. When the huge figure, brought to bay, turned to face them he fought madly, desperately, bellowing forth his anguished defiance all the while, and it took the help of the guards of the red room to overpower him and carry him away in spite of the weakening tortures to which he had been subjected. As, panting and breathless, they carried the lunging, struggling figure out into the corridor and back to the torture chamber, Isabel turned to clasp Mariam in her arms.

"Let us pray, dear," she wept. "It may be our last moment of freedom in this life," and the two girls knelt in humble supplication.

This was only for a moment, and then just within range of Mariam's eyes, a door in the opposite wall swung to one side, and, in a narrow opening, thus revealed, stood the gray muffled figure of a priest. As he

PRINCE IZON

drew back his cowl the girls with a thrill of thankfulness recognized Zeno.

"Hurry! Hurry for your lives!" he said. Mariam flew to him but Isabel had sunk moaning to the floor as another scream of anguish came from the torture chamber.

Zeno raised her and tenderly supported by Mariam, together they entered a narrow passage in darkness, Zeno feeling his way along the wall. Presently he stopped and, reaching up, said,

"This is the place."

Climbing to a passage about his own height above the one they were in, he reached down and with much labor drew up the girls. Proceeding in the same single file they soon saw light ahead and suddenly, to their intense relief, Mariam and Isabel entered a large cavern-like room lit by the moonlight entering by an opening overlooking the river.

"Love o' mine," said a well-known voice, and the next moment Isabel was crying hysterically in the arms of Black Eagle. In reply to her gasping inquiries, he said,

"Another devilish trick of that demon, Topeltzin;

THE RED ROOM

I have been here over an hour with Tepultac, waiting for you."

"Then," asked Mariam, "what poor creature was that being tortured?" Zeno was silent for a moment.

"It was Captain Helox," he said solemnly.

The five were silent with awe and horror until presently Zeno said,

"We are safe for the present. This room is the ancient and lost entrance to the inside spiral stairway leading to the top of the teocolli. Even Topeltzin does not know of the passage by which we reached it."

"How do you know that?" inquired Black Eagle, "for it is our only safety from his pursuit."

"Why, this way. At the place where we climbed up, the other passage turns at right angles leading into the garden. Topeltzin and myself had been searching for the lost passage and I was following him, lighting the way with a torch. Topeltzin reached the angle, turned it and went on, as the mouth of the upper passage is hid by the rock formation, but I noticed that the smoke from the torch suddenly left the ceiling where it had rolled along and disappeared straight up and ahead. I knew what this draft meant but quickly fol-

PRINCE IZON

lowed Topeltzin. When he had abandoned the search in disgust, I returned and found my way here. Oh, there were crafty high priests before Topeltzin's time."

Black Eagle then explained that after leaving them in the balcony overlooking the banquet, he and Tepultac had communicated through Azra and Zilpan the dread news of Izon's failure to escape and his coming fate, to the Pearl City. Guided by Zeno they had come hither and Zeno had gone to the red room for the girls, intending, if necessary, to summon them to his assistance, but, as events proved, this was not required.

Zeno now reminded them all of their need of rest for the fateful to-morrow.

The girls were exhausted and soon fell asleep on a pallet of fur skins screened off in a rocky alcove.

Black Eagle and Zeno disposed themselves on skins in the centre of the floor, but Tepultac sat in the opening overlooking the river thinking of his wrongs at the hands of Topeltzin, and planning for his coming vengeance on the morrow.

CHAPTER XXXIII
AT SUNRISE

BEFORE the gray dawn of the morning had broken, Tepultac, who knew no sleep but had been busy with plans for vengeance, aroused the girls.

"The time has come," he said.

A spring of water trickled into a rocky basin, and, after quick ablutions, the girls, in response to a call, went in to where the men where completing their preparations. Black Eagle they found in complete Spanish armor which Tepultac had secured for him during the night and which he was now busily helping the chieftain to adjust. Black Eagle was armed with a remarkable weapon, — a long spear, the head of which had been removed and replaced by a large bowie knife that Professor Raymon had given him years before. He also carried a Spanish sword for Prince Izon, and now Zeno handed a dagger to each of the girls, with the grim comment that at the very last they might be glad to turn them upon themselves.

Without further parley he led the way to the base of the circular stairway. He turned impatiently as he put his foot upon the first step to find that, as by one accord, the four who were to accompany him had fallen to their knees in final supplication before facing the gravest crisis of their lives. For a moment Zeno pondered, frowning. His apostasy from Topeltzin had been upon personal grounds, and to the matter of religion he had given but little thought. Tepultac he did not heed, for he knew the revenge that burned within him. As for Black Eagle, he was a strong man in whom Zeno found rugged elements that upon the surface dissociated him from the idea of worship; but the pure, earnest faith of the two girls, the beauty of simple trust that he found in their upturned devout faces, impressed him so that he too, though scarcely knowing what he did nor why he did it, knelt with them and partook of the blessing that these children of the Father invoked for their undertaking. Silently then they trudged up the endless circle, with many a halt for breath and many a pause for wonder at the skill of the early priests, who had raised this temple to their deity. The dawn was breaking now, and through the

AT SUNRISE

small interstices that had been constructed here and there the dim day filtered in enough to show them the dizzy height which they still must ascend, its pinnacle lost in a tiny point of light.

At last they found themselves within the body of the gigantic statue of Tezcatlipoca upon the apex of the teocolli. Zeno and Tepultac at once passed out of the concealed opening in one of the deep folds in the garments of the statue. They were clad in their priestly robes, and as it was customary for two or more priests to ascend the teocolli early in the morning, to keep replenished the fire that burned always before the statue and to see that all within the temple was in final readiness for the sacrifice, their early presence would seem but natural.

It was now a mere matter of waiting, and the girls looked out in awed admiration through the numerous apertures that, to all outside appearance, formed a part of the carved and fretted decoration of the robes of the statue. With the breaking dawn, the mist that lay in the canyon, its surface rolling in gentle undulations like a vast long lake of filmy clouds, quivered as if with coming life. Temple and statue faced the eastern sun, and when the huge orb presently appeared, rising slowly and majestically, a great flaming copper ball, above the cliffs at the head of the upper canyon, the whole bosom of this undulating mist gleamed with a golden iridescence that changed to a thousand pure unsurpassable hues, while still retaining its golden undersheen. Great moving billows of violet, of blue, of green, of yellow, of orange, of red, came sweeping down the canyon, one after the other, blending and melting, each into the one preceding it, like a gigantic fairy phantasmagoria, borrowing color from the walls of the canyon, from the masses of vegetation, from the vault of heaven, and turning these and the gold from the great lamp of day into spectra more clear and pure than the refraction from any prism of crystal, while at the same time more soft and evanescent than the tints of the most delicate rainbow. Amethyst, sapphire, turquoise, opal, emerald, topaz, ruby, lilac, iris, primrose, daffodil, marigold, carnation, rose — mauve, syenite, vert, ochre, cadmium, vermilion, carmine, all came trooping down in their elusive, bewildering array until, with startling swiftness upon the higher rise of the sun, the gorgeous Pageant of Aurora suddenly disappeared.

AT SUNRISE

Now, as the sun rose still higher and drew up that intangible body of opalescent vapor from the depths of the canyon, the beauties of the great chasm itself were displayed in all their stupendous grandeur. Building after building, palace after palace, of the Red City were revealed and stood forth in their bold beauty, a new revelation of the master genius Topeltzin had displayed in the use of limitless wealth and limitless power. But the rising mist too illuminated one more object that for the girls and Black Eagle had more vital interest, more personal significance, than all this vast panorama, and this was the golden cross, which, springing into life so vividly as the sunlight struck upon it that it seemed like a heaven-sent covenant of hope and succor, stood majestically glittering where it towered above the church in the Pearl City. As a symbol of all that they worshipped, of all that was best and purest and noblest in their lives, they gave to it their silent adoration.

CHAPTER XXXIV

THE BLESSING OF THE TROOPS

LONG before daylight the temple plaza of the Pearl City had been lit up by hundreds of torches in the flaring yellow light of which the troops of Luxtol had assembled. From every street battalion after battalion had debouched into the plaza where the proper military formations were quickly effected. There was no noise or confusion or excitement. Stern, deep, earnestness animated all; even the commands were given in low tones. Presently in serried ranks and filling the entire plaza, the army stood in close formation facing the church front where on the summit of the steps stood Don Raymon Navarez. Near him, but concealed in the shadow of the arched doorway stood Zilpan. While he had not been summoned to join the ranks as a fighter he knew that the purpose of this early massing of the soldiers was to have them attend divine services before going into battle, and impelled partly by curiosity and partly by a feeling that he too should participate in the blessing to be bestowed, he had come to the church.

BLESSING THE TROOPS

Zilpan's new allegiance to Christianity was not based on belief but was solely the result of Topeltzin's treatment of Azra. But ever since his repudiation of the high priest, a vague unrest had seized him and a desire to see and hear the Christian ceremonials in the temple had overmastered him.

The battalion officers, headed by Tezcotzin, finally reported in turn to Don Raymon that their formations were complete and at his signal the church doors were opened and through them the warriors marched with lowered arms. Every available man in Luxtol had gladly responded to the call and the huge edifice was filled with the marching thousands. Zilpan followed the last company of soldiers but found the nave so crowded that in order to get a good view of the sanctuary, he ascended the stairs leading to the organ loft. Half-way up was a landing which commanded a view of the entire scene, and upon this he halted. Vast and dim, the body of the church was illuminated by only a few torches, but the golden altar was ablaze with light and to the deep notes of the organ Father Zolcoma and his assistants conducted the devotions.

Zilpan was profoundly impressed with their deep

solemnity, where every word, every movement to the slightest gesture, had a significance that two thousand years had only intensified. His gaze leaving the sanctuary for a moment swept over the sea of upturned faces; those of thousands of kneeling soldiers, each as a devout Christian realizing that the next few hours might be his last on earth or, in the event of defeat and capture, that a horrible torture and final death under the obsidian knife awaited him.

The most solemn part of the ceremony now drew nigh and at a low-voiced command from Don Raymon the entire army arose from their knees, and with a sound like the distant rumble of a coming storm, arms were presented in honor of the elevation — a sound followed by the thunder-like crash of the weapons as they were grounded on the tiled pave. Zilpan noted how the vastness of the dim interior rendered the altar more dazzling. As the deep organ chords to which the building trembled, swelled around him, he descended the stairs and, impelled by an irresistible impulse, slowly pushed his way through the crowd until he reached the rail of the sanctuary, where he prostrated himself in adoration to the Host that shone high in air, throned in light. At the conclusion of the ritual Father Zolcoma ascended the pulpit.

"Beloved Christians," he said, "the most momentous day in our history is dawning. This day it will be decided whether Christ or Tezcatlipoca will reign in the hearts of the people in the canyon cities. For centuries, our Lord has permitted Luxtol and Ixtol to grow side by side and both wax great. With us vice is unknown and peace and contentment prevail; with them, the reverse is the case and the Red City has become a den of iniquity. But, quite recently, the powers that rule Ixtol have gained a great advantage over us and in a few hours our beloved prince will be sacrificed in honor of their gods, and the maidens subjected to a fate worse than death, unless our deeds and prayers can prevent it. Not content with the destruction of the bodies of his victims, Topeltzin has tried with diabolical cunning first to destroy their souls. Each one has been tempted in the most insidious way but, thanks be to God, each one has triumphed over the wiles of the Evil One except the Indian chieftain who yielded for the moment. The two maidens, rather than yield, are facing a horrible fate while living and a dreadful death as the culmination! Against your beloved prince, however, has the most tremendous attack been made. His mere butchery on the teocolli will not satisfy Topeltzin — whose real aim is to insult our God and our faith. And now, beloved ones, comes the working of that law of compensation which I have so often expounded to you from this pulpit: 'You reap as you sow.' Prince Izon, as you all know, had led a blameless life — his character built up so that in this awful crisis he has triumphed; but his friend the Indian, not having had this self-discipline, fell into the trap prepared for him. He soon repented however, and to-day, if I mistake not, he will gloriously redeem himself. The hour is approaching when the decisive conflict will be waged. On the teocolli and at the Red City gates it will be Christians against Pagans; and we, who believe that not a feather drops from the swallow's wing without His consent, will know that while our foes are being inspired by the Evil One, that their Creator as well as ours is looking on and will not desert us!

"Soldiers of Luxtol, you are therefore going to fight for a glorious cause, your God and your prince! And now in the absence of that prince your hereditary com-

BLESSING THE TROOPS

mander, I, by direction of the Council of State, have appointed Don Raymon Navarez your chief, who will lead you in this conflict.

"In the days of the Conquest a Spanish knight by an act of heroism but at the sacrifice of his own life, saved several of his comrades who were about to be sacrificed on the teocolli of old Mexico. His sword and armor have been preserved as noble relics, and to Don Raymon — as a worthy successor to him — I now present them."

As he spoke attendants approached Don Raymon who had been kneeling in the sanctuary, and when he arose, they adjusted the shining armor upon him. "This sword," continued Father Zolcoma, descending from the pulpit, and presenting the weapon to Don Raymon, "was never drawn without cause, nor sheathed without honor. Accept it, Señor, in that spirit!" and as the army presented arms Don Raymon, kneeling, received the sword.

Again the tempest-like sound of the "Present arms!" followed by the deep rumble of their grounding, shook the temple as Don Raymon gave his knightly salute.

"Now, soldiers of Luxtol," cried Father Zolcoma,

raising his arms in supplication, his voice, ringing like a clarion, filling the vast edifice, "Receive the blessing that I am empowered to bestow. Go forth upon your glorious mission with highest hopes and bravest hearts and may the same God who divided the water of the sea for his own people and closed those waters over their enemies, guide you to victory this day!

"Destined avengers of your brethren and ancestors who, captured by the pagans and who rather than repudiate their God, suffered torture and martyrdom under the obsidian knife, I bless you in the name of the down-trodden past! Coming rescuers of your prince and his companions, the victims of pagan lust and hate, I bless you in the name of the dawning future! Invoking the power of the Most High for aid in this, your first united assault upon the forces of Satan, O champions of the Cross and defenders of the Faith, I bless you in the name of the Omnipotent Father, Son, and Holy Spirit! I bless you and you shall be blessed!"

CHAPTER XXXV
A SOLEMN REPROOF

THE watchers in the statue now noted that already there was a stir in the plaza below. Its bustle came up to them through the rarified atmosphere with clear distinctness, and a thrill came over the girls as they realized what all this unwonted agitation meant, a thrill that was in no wise lessened when Zeno called in to them, tapping it smartly as he spoke,

"This is the sacrificial stone."

Isabel and Mariam shuddered as their attention was called to the stone, directly beneath them, upon which Izon was to die. They had been looking calmly out over it, even down upon it, without realizing the terrible part it was intended to play in the tragedy to come. It was a huge, elliptical block of solid granite, carved richly around its circumference with symbolic figures, the Aztec gods of life and death. In the top of the stone was a groove that had attracted their curious speculation, but now it came upon them with the shock of a vital blow

PRINCE IZON

that this gutter was to allow the torrent of human blood to flow down. It was backed up against the feet of the idol, practically open for the front two-thirds of its circumference, and from this height the quivering heart of Izon was to be held up as the supreme climax of the hideous ceremony. Gazing at the stone in fascination for a time they were glad to turn away and look beyond it, to follow, down the side of the teocolli, the winding pathway by which Izon must presently ascend.

Those who have seen pictures of the teocolli of Tezcatlipoca in the City of Mexico can form a slight idea of this one, but a better impression can be gained from the most commonly known picture of the tower of Babel; for the teocolli of the Red City was much taller and narrower at the base and much more ornate in its continuous parapet than any of those made by the older Aztecs in Mexico, the small base and immense proportionate height of this one being forced by the limited area. It was built of stone, and an inclined plane ran steeply around its four sides, winding from the plaza in front of Topeltzin's palace to the top, which, standing out as it did at the very edge of the

A SOLEMN REPROOF

precipice, formed the dominant landmark of the Red City.

The drum upon the tower top solemnly boomed out its summons and the populace began to pour out from everywhere. The plaza filled as if by magic. The palace guards marched down the road along the cliffside to the distant wall, to reinforce the troops already there. From the height of the teocolli the watchers could now see another slowly moving line rounding the cliff from the Pearl City far up the canyon. The ceaseless profound basso of the river came solemnly up to them, and now, upon the monotonous undertone which seemed to be filled with present menace, there suddenly burst a shriller sound, a fanfare of trumpets. The central doors of the palace, swung only upon state occasions, had opened. Preceded by trumpeters, a band of priests came slowly forth and the chant that arose up to the great statue was one that had a savage triumph in it. Following the priests came a band of flower girls gay with the sacrificial blossoms of crimson, and their clear sopranos rose in response. Mariam suddenly clutched her hand to her heart and bent forth eagerly.

PRINCE IZON

Just behind the girls came Izon, clad in a simple robe of white, bearing himself erectly and proudly. Tears started into the eyes of Mariam, as she felt the pitying clasp of Isabel's arms about her waist.

"Oh, Isabel," she cried, "if the knife pierces his heart, I too shall die. Is there no help and no hope? Has God deserted us?"

As if in solemn reproof, there came one of those acoustic phenomena which are among the greatest wonders of the canyon. Down the mighty chasm rolled the sounds of thousands of voices chanting afar.

"Kyrie Eleison! Christe Eleison!"

was being reverently sung in the response to the solemn services in behalf of Izon by those people of Luxtol who had not gone forth that morning to battle.

No note of unbelief broke the harmony of the hymn for mercy, the appeal "O Lord, save him! O Christ, save him!" which was sung that morning in the church of the Christians, to be reëchoed from the canyon walls of the north to their towering mates on the south. Swelled by the organ to a grand diapason, it burst the confines of the quivering edifice and rolled from crag to crag, filling the canyon with its reverberations of

A SOLEMN REPROOF

solemn supplication. It swept over the soldiers of the Pearl City, and those of the Red, massed behind their respective ramparts, lulling for a time their fierce shouts of defiance as they prepared to grapple in deadly conflict. Augmented to a tremendous chorus by the Christian host, who, like the Crusaders, adopted the call as their battle-cry, it transformed their enthusiasm into the exultation of coming victory, while it chilled their pagan foes, enervated by their debaucheries of the preceding night. It reached the boisterous crowd in the plaza and awed into silence their bloodthirsty jubilations. It thrilled with courage and hope the hearts of the trembling girls on the teocolli, and it inspired Black Eagle to coming deeds of invincible might, as with implicit faith in the divine mercy, they joined in the appeal that ascended to the empyrean and besieged the gates of heaven!

The gage of battle was cast; it was Christianity against Paganism — God against Tezcatlipoca!

CHAPTER XXXVI
ON THE TEOCOLLI—PAGANISM

WITH what trepidation the watchers, sheltered within the very statue which represented all in this world that was of enmity to them, gazed down upon the slowly winding procession that now ascended the teocolli! The band of flower girls still strewed their red blossoms before the feet of Izon, as they reached the summit, each flower a reminder to him of the approaching moment of agony, if he had chosen so to regard it. So far as all outward appearances were concerned, however, Izon suffered no anguish. His face was calm, and his clear eyes looked ever steadfastly upward. The features of Topeltzin, on the other hand, had no such expression. His was the first head to rise to the level of the parapet, and as his evil countenance appeared the girls involuntarily started back in affright from the holes through which they had been gazing, lest his piercing eyes might penetrate and discover them. His face was drawn by the passions to

ON THE TEOCOLLI

which he had given vent through the night; hours had been spent in hunting the girls and Black Eagle, and the downfall of half his purpose had put him in a mood of savage, smouldering fury.

With no suspicion of the three pairs of eyes that were watching him from within the statue he stopped before the sacrificial stone with a low obeisance to the huge image. The flower girls came next and surrounded the stone with garlands, then they fell back on either side, forming a lane for those to come later. Izon now came within the range of vison. It was with a mocking smile that he bowed in answer to Topeltzin's bow, and Mariam for the first time realized the strength of these men. They were mortal enemies, and one was within a few moments to die at the hand of the other, yet they saluted each other in apparent courtesy even while they glared defiance into each other's eyes.

If Topeltzin had hoped to see Izon cowed and despairing he was doomed to disappointment; as at the banquet there was forced the same reluctant admiration in his cruel nature for the proud prince who met death as calmly as an invitation to a feast. Stirred by some impulse, Topeltzin held forth his hand and, taking

PRINCE IZON

Izon's, assisted him to mount the sacrificial stone, where, elevated above all the others he could, for the last time, look down upon the Red City, upon the peaceful canyon, and far away to where the cross of Christianity was burnished into radiance by the morning sunlight. As his eyes rested upon this, Izon's lips moved for a moment in silent prayer and then, his soul clear with his Maker, he cast about him the apparently indifferent look of an idle spectator upon the preparations for his own death.

The cordon of priests now filed past. Each abased himself before Tezcatlipoca and then marched into the small temple opposite the statue. Topeltzin standing before the stone and Izon standing upon it, were motionless, the very incarnation of the doomsman and the doomed.

Deep within the prince, however, was the torment of uncertainty. Where were Black Eagle and the girls? No commotion had arisen to indicate their discovery. What had happened to them! He had heard no word or trace of them since the night before, when he had been dragged away from the banquet dais, and his heart was filled with gloomy conjectures though

ON THE TEOCOLLI

he allowed no trace of them to show upon his face. If he must go to his death he would go like a man, nor let this arch-tormentor see a qualm of fear. It might only have added to his distress to have known that where he stood he was near enough for Mariam almost to have reached out and touched him, had there been an opening large enough. She was nearly frantic with a desire to but touch his robe, and in her bosom there came a sudden pain so violent that it was like the pang of a knife stroke. Within the bend of her strained arms was an actual ache, borne of the desire to clasp him in those arms and to hide him away from that cruel curved blade which Topeltzin bore aloft as the insignia of office.

Slowly the flower girls took up the strains of a farewell chant, and at its conclusion, their eyes suffused with tears, began to countermarch down the way of death, while Mariam and Isabel were silently weeping as if their hearts would break. Black Eagle, however, was far differently affected. All this ceremonial drove home to him the fact of the deep seriousness of these priests and warned him of the tremendous odds against himself and Izon. No sound escaped him but a deeper

PRINCE IZON

breath, a tightening here and there of his armor buckles, a firmer grasp of his spear shaft alone showed his comprehension of the dread task before him. The six priests, three on either side of the sacrificial stone, who had been left to guard Izon, now took up the burden of the same chant, and the response was made within the temple, where the other priests were holding the ceremonial that preceded each sacrifice, and these Topeltzin now joined. It was but a few minutes later when he emerged, followed by his entire band. The priests, wearing about their necks huge rolled collars, now loosened these rolls and, the capes dropping to the floor, they were all clad in scarlet from head to foot. This was the signal for which Azra from her tower had been watching with straining eyes. It was the moment when the battle could begin at the gates and she flew down to her prison room to transfer the news to Zilpan. Again sounded the dirge, that, wailing and moaning its doleful cadences, had at the last moment broken the stoicism of more than one victim. When it ceased and as Topeltzin with a wolfish smile approached, there came down the canyon, an answering cry —

ON THE TEOCOLLI

"*Credo in unum Deum, Patrem Omnipotentem, factorem coeli et terra!*"

Topeltzin paused as if stung. Once more the marvellous acoustics of the canyon had wafted to the teocolli a hymn from the Christian church. When he comprehended what it was that he had heard his face became livid with rage. He wheeled back once more to the direction of the rising sun, and throwing up both his brawny arms, shrieked out, more like an imprecation than the grave ceremonial it was intended to be:

"O Tezcatlipoca, to whose beams we owe light and life and all that blooms and blossoms upon the face of the earth, accept this crimson offering of your humble slaves!"

Wheeling abruptly he sprang to the sacrificial stone and ordered the priests to whom this duty fell:

"Bare him for the sacrifice!"

Izon, having no hint as yet whether his friends had failed him or not, still poised himself for such resistance as he might make. He was no willing victim, bound by superstition to accept this as his fate, and to the last moment he intended to sell his life as dearly as he

PRINCE IZON

might, since there was small chance to save it. He was unarmed, and the priests that now closed on the stone, with sleeves folded back to the elbows, had sharp daggers at their belts. Topeltzin's own muscular arm was bared, and the horrible obsidian knife was upraised.

A piercing scream sounded in the interior of the statue of Tezcatlipoca. Mariam had fainted.

CHAPTER XXXVII

ON THE TEOCOLLI—HEROISM

THE screams from within the statue was drowned by a yell of rage and mortal anguish from without. The scarlet-robed figure nearest Topeltzin had suddenly sprung up to confront him, and crying in a loud voice, "I, too, believe in one God!" had thrust a dagger at his heart; but the high priest, quick as a tiger, had met this attack half way and with his obsidian knife had delivered the death blow to his assailant. It was poor Tepultac, who, thus balked of his revenge, gave a cry as he sank to the stone floor. Confusion ensued. The surprised priests stood aghast, watching the brief struggle, and in that moment a tall figure in armor that glittered in the sunlight suddenly appeared on the stone from behind the statue. Into Izon's hands he thrust a sword and a knife, and then instantly and terrifically attacked the priests with the long spear upon which was bound the bowie knife. With lightning-like quickness, he lunged it forward, and at every thrust it

PRINCE IZON entered the body of a priest who went down as though struck by an electric bolt.

In the first onslaught he had inflicted a slight gash upon the knife arm of Topeltzin, who, with imprecations, jumped away, and it was but a moment until the two, Black Eagle attacking the outer circle and Izon doing swift killing with his sword and dagger at closer range, had cleared a space of several feet in front of the stone, the priests, in fact, cowering back to the parapet. In that same time the forces of the Pearl City, led by Don Raymon, stormed the gates of the Red City, so that simultaneously a desperate conflict between the pagans and the Christians had begun on the teocolli and at the outpost of Ixtol.

For a moment the surprise of the onslaught and the wound that he had himself received had taken Topeltzin off his guard, but with such a man no loss of control could be lasting, and quickly recovering, with loud command he ordered his priests to the fray. Under the lash of his will they dashed for the stone in frenzy, but in that brief time the two friends had taken up, naturally, the best order of defence. The sacrificial stone being against the pedestal of the statue prevented

ON THE TEOCOLLI

an attack from the rear. Black Eagle standing beside Izon, thrust out and beyond at the outer circle of priests with snake-like rapidity, turning from side to side and keeping at bay the major portion of the assailants, while Izon, in a crouching position, his left arm wrapped in part of his robe to use as a shield, his left hand grasping the dagger, and his right arm and shoulder bare, was wielding his sword with a swiftness and dexterity that made its flashes seem like gleams of swiftly recurrent lightning. They were like demi-gods, these two stalwart men in their superb courage and their prowess, and the girls within watched with bated breath, bemoaning their helplessness in the terrific conflict, praying by turns for the safety of their knights, and for the success of the armed forces which a deep booming sound from below told them had begun the storming of the gates.

Fiercer the conflict grew. The priests, like bloodthirsty tigers, pressed around the stone with howls of rage, mingled with screams of anguish as the stricken ones sank to rise no more. Several times some of their number succeeded in clambering upon one side of the stone while the fighting was on the front, but both Black

PRINCE IZON

Eagle and Izon kept constantly turning and twisting, wheeling for a fresh opponent in the same instant that a desperate stroke was delivered to another, fighting like demons, the bowie knife on the end of the spear darting in and out like a tongue of fatal flame, the sword whirling like a flashing circle of death.

Out from the visor of Black Eagle there now came a savage war-cry. His blood was boiling in his veins, throbbing in his temples, tingling in his finger-tips; his heart was thumping strongly against his breast, his breath was heaving from the bottom of his expanded lungs, and his whole gigantic frame quivered with the joy of battle. His cry was a note of triumph, of glee, of savage glory in the conflict, for back through the generations, each marked with the lust and prowess of battle, had come all their savage ferocity. This moment was the keenest ecstasy that had ever entered into his life, and just behind him, watching every movement with bated breath, his natural mate, now more sure of the fact than ever since she had known him, was herself stirred by that trace of Indian blood in her veins, and she almost screamed out in mad exultation as the crimson-robed wolves went down before his mighty

The Fight on the Teocolli

ON THE TEOCOLLI

strokes. Mariam, revived but still faint and weakened, pressed against the pierced stone in front of her, her lips parted in terror, her eyes distended in wild fear that each blow might be the one that would strike Izon down. In her, while she could not but admire the strength and dexterity and courage of Izon, there was no exhilaration in this horrible conflict. She would far rather have accepted him in peace and walked with him throughout life under rose-hung bowers; but not so Isabel. For every successful stroke that Black Eagle gave, she felt a thrill of fierce pride, and the blood of her own warrior ancestors stirred within her so that she longed to bear her share in the brunt of the battle.

The priests were screaming and cursing but no sound came from Izon or Black Eagle, save that one war-whoop. With teeth clinched and eyes blazing they whirled and thrust with automatic precision, and with every thrust a flowing red gash was left. Now there was a third figure near the sacrificial stone, a scarlet-clad figure, fighting with them, wielding his short knife with terrific fury and attempting to force his way across to where Topeltzin urged on his hordes and watched, with a cool and calculating eye, for a chance to himself spring in with a quick, decisive blow. The cowl of this new ally was thrown back but the girls could not see his face. They knew well enough, however, that this was Zeno, who, warmed by the conflict and the heroism of the two principals, was fighting now in open battle for them. Against the force of numbers the three defenders had but one advantage. The priests were armed only with short knives and stood upon a lower level; moreover they were befuddled by the orgy following the banquet and incapable of concerted action. The length of Izon's sword and the much greater length of Black Eagle's spear gave them a chance for their lives, and they made such terrific use of this chance that soon the entire space around the stone for several feet was filled with dead and dying priests, many of them writhing and screaming in death's agony, all of them covered with blood, thus forming between the besieged and the fanatics, a rolling, slippery barrier over which the attacking priests had to pass before they could strike.

While the din of the conflict was at its height a shadow fell over the scene. Looking up with a quick appreciation of every circumstance which, no matter how trivial, might have a bearing upon the outcome, Isabel

ON THE TEOCOLLI

saw hovering over the temple a black cloud that had come slowly above them from the lower canyon. In the tenseness of the action upon the top of the teocolli and in the excitement of that other attack at the gates of the city, no one had paid any attention to this until suddenly a deep roll of thunder reverberated through the canyon, its detonation at this height being almost ear-splitting.

CHAPTER XXXVIII

ON THE TEOCOLLI—DESPERATION

THE clap of thunder scarcely disturbed the priests about the sacrificial stone. Crazed with blood lust they were like wild animals, all their senses in abeyance except the one mad desire to slay. One after another of the red-robed fanatics rushed over his dead comrades, only to meet the knife or the sword, to throw up his hands, to shriek, to sink back to rise no more. Until now Izon had uttered no sound. Every atom of his being had been concentrated on the one mighty exertion to kill; to plunge his weapon into the head or breast of the foes who swarmed before him. Suddenly the space in front of the stone was clear, except for the hideously writhing mass of wounded priests, over which the living hesitated to charge. As he noted this, as the conviction suddenly came to him that Black Eagle and himself would win, a magnificent exultation possessed him. All his rage against Topeltzin, of necessity suppressed until this moment, blazed forth. Pointing

ON THE TEOCOLLI

his dripping blade at the high priest, "Murderer of women!" he cried, "poltroon high priest, skulking there! Give that knife to a man not afraid to use it, you slinking coward!" Topeltzin shuddered between rage and humiliation. Never before in the traditions of Ixtol had a victim resisted in this way. Never before had a high priest been thus degraded, and that he, he who had counted on this scene to be his crowning triumph, should be thus reviled, was maddening. But Topeltzin in some respects was truly great, and now restrained himself from rushing upon Izon.

He had waited in vain for an opening, holding himself poised to spring in at the first opportunity and to himself deliver the blow that would give the victim his quietus; but now he called half a dozen of the priests to one side and held a short conference. After talking with them crisply he pondered for a second and then suddenly pointed his finger at one of the priests.

"You, Axama!" he directed sharply.

The one addressed as Axama folded his hands across his breast, bowing with piteous resignation to his death sentence, and then the entire party went around to the front of the stone. They waited for an opening in that wavering mob and made a rush, but, quick as they were, Black Eagle was ready and his terrific spear-thrust met Axama fair in the breast. That was precisely the action for which Axama had been prepared. He saw that thrust coming but did not try to evade it; instead, he threw himself forward upon it with all his strength, and, grasping the spear shaft with a convulsive movement, helped the thrust with his own exertion. To Black Eagle's dismay he found that the knife was buried in the priest's breast, and now he realized the purpose of this self-sacrifice; it was to render the terrible weapon useless. With a horrible yell, Axama strove even in the very midst of this mortal stroke to drag his slayer with him down from the stone. He had laid down his life to make this opening, and Topeltzin urged on his priests to take advantage of it.

Only Izon's sword and dagger and Zeno's short knife now remained to stem the onrush, and, while they were performing what amounted to miracles with these weapons, it was evident that the fight would soon be over without Black Eagle's aid. Izon was sorely pressed, while the roll about his left arm received thrust after thrust, and he was only saved from one vicious

ON THE TEOCOLLI

stroke by Zeno receiving the knife in his left shoulder where it remained sticking to the hilt. Black Eagle in the meantime had been tugging and straining to regain his spear, and now that savage strain within him that had driven him to maniacal glory in this conflict, impelled him to a deed of titanic strength. Dropping suddenly upon one knee and using the other as a fulcrum, with a tremendous effort he lifted Axama up and flung him over his head past the statue, where he slipped from the knife, falling out over the parapet and hurtling over and over in the air, down and down, clearing the teocolli and falling, a bruised and broken mass, on the stones of the plaza among the terrified people.

So appalled were the priests by this feat that for a moment they fell back, and even after Black Eagle had whirled his spear to position ready for another lunge, they were motionless, except Topeltzin who, now losing all self-control, became a raving maniac. His frenzied roar recalled the priests to themselves and once more they swarmed forward for a final charge. With a sudden crouching motion one of them slipped under Izon's guard and struck at his breast. For the second time a scream came from within the statue and though Zeno

PRINCE IZON

had lunged sideways in time to save Izon, the damage was done.

Topeltzin's quick ear had located that scream, and, rushing to the back of the statue he saw the opening from which Black Eagle had emerged. Into this he now darted, and with a hoarse yell of passion he clutched both the girls and drew them forth before they had even time for thought of resistance. His appearance was so horrible that the girls were paralyzed with terror and did not for a moment even think of the daggers that had been given them. His robe was torn and blood-stained, while his face, half-covered with blood, was that of a beast, and, as he glared upon them with vengeful, blood-shot eyes, they were so terrified that the strength seemed to desert their bodies, leaving them limp and helpless. Blinded with fury he suddenly jerked them around to the parapet and shoved Mariam into the arms of the nearest priest. With a jerk of his hand Topeltzin motioned the priest to follow him, and, lifting Isabel, he poised to plunge her over the abyss below, down into that terrible depth where the river in the bottom of the canyon yawned ever for more victims.

Topeltzin's murderous purpose was a double one.

ON THE TEOCOLLI

He intended not only to glut the rage that was in his heart against these girls who had so far escaped him, but also to distract the attention of Izon and Black Eagle, and this last purpose was already accomplished. The scream of Isabel as she was swept from her feet caught the attention of both men, and for an instant they stopped, transfixed by this new horror, while in that moment the priests sprang forward from all sides at once. As Topeltzin lifted her, Isabel turned her head in Black Eagle's direction and tried to wave him a last good-bye, for she felt that her hour had come, but as she turned she saw him spring to the edge of the sacrificial stone, paying no attention to the horde that were thronging around him, and hurl his spear at Topeltzin. It was a master-stroke, swift and straight as an arrow, for the side of the high priest, where the blade passed under his arm, badly wounding him, the shaft splintering against the parapet. With a groan Topeltzin sank down, carrying Isabel with him, but she felt that his clasp of her was loose, and she had barely touched the ground when she sprang to her feet and rushed to Mariam. She now had her dagger in her hand, though she could not have told how it came there, and with all the force that was in her, she plunged it into the body of the priest who was at that very moment swinging Mariam for the throw. The blow went home, but even as he sank, two other priests seized the girls, eager to carry out Topeltzin's plan, and again they were lifted to be cast over the parapet.

Mariam's appealing eyes were fixed on Izon, but he was beset by three of his assailants who had closed in upon him, and he could not lift a hand to save them. Black Eagle drew his knife and threw it at Isabel's captor, then turned to force his way through to her. Isabel, her head turned so that she must perforce take in the stretch from the plaza up the canyon, saw an immense rabble running toward the teocolli at hot speed. They were the soldiers of Topeltzin in wild disorder, and after them, like an avenging Nemesis, came the soldiers of the Pearl City. The latter had carried the gate and were sweeping its defenders before them. But, even if they stormed and won the teocolli it would take them half an hour to scale it, and their coming would not be in time to save any of the four to whom Doom had already opened his gaunt arms.

CHAPTER XXXIX

THE BATTLE AT THE GATES

THAT had been a terrific conflict at the gates. Midway between the Pearl and Red Cities, walls had been erected across the wide shelf of the cliff which formed a highway between the domains. Each wall was guarded night and day by its own defenders, and between the walls was a neutral space upon which no adherent of either side set foot, except sometimes when the guards, establishing a truce, met for the rough games to which their class was addicted. Now, however, both walls were doubly guarded. Topeltzin, whose spy system was an intricate and wonderful thing, knew of the assault that was to be made against his forces and had massed them all under command of Gautemotzin behind the Red City gates, but he had caused the news to be sent, by direct messenger to Father Zolcoma himself, that any signal for attack before Izon ascended the teocolli would be the signal for Izon's death. After that, no force on earth could save the prince, he thought.

PRINCE IZON

Far different from that of the Christians had been the pagan preparation for the battle. Knowing that the long night of debauchery in which his soldiers had indulged would have its inevitable effect on the morrow, Topeltzin had issued vast quantities of the strongest liquors to the troops and in a half-drunken, yet evilly inspirited harangue, Gautemotzin had aroused them to reckless courage by promising the unlimited loot and despoilment of the treasures and people of the Pearl City as their prize.

It was a long column and an earnest one that had marched out of Luxtol and had come to halt within the shelter of its own outpost wall, and toward the rear of the army was a most unusual and un-warlike object. It was a black palanquin with shuttered sides, borne by relays of four men each, and within its light-excluded walls sat a young man with pale, drawn face and white, slender hands that covered his eyes. As the column neared the gates he was speaking softly but in an intense tone, as if conversing earnestly with some one who was there by his side but unseen.

"Nearer and still nearer, O soul of my soul!" he was saying. "In the midst of death I am coming to thee and to life, after these two weary years. And now, beloved, again what tidings?"

He became silent now and sat strained as if listening intently, but presently he tapped upon the little door at his side. It was opened by a soldier who peered in curiously at the wide, dreaming eyes of Zilpan.

"Go tell Don Raymon that Prince Izon is now ascending the teocolli," he directed, and the soldier, reserving for the coming race his constant wonderment at this uncanny puzzle, dashed away to the front of the column, leaving another to take his place and close the door upon the pale mystic.

Far off in Topeltzin's palace, high up in her black apartment, sat Azra, her face aglow with excitement, her waxen cheeks tinted with the first trace of color that had been upon them for many months. Zilpan was coming! With that marvellous sense which had been developed within her, she had followed every step of his progress and it seemed as if each minute's lessening of the space between them had infused her with new life, had quickened her long-starved love again into rich blossoming. Upon all sides of the tower in the room above opened out tiny windows, from one of which she could see the top of the teocolli; but as the glaring light of this apartment was too distracting for communion with that absent twin soul of hers, she was constantly running up and down the narrow stairway, one moment to see what was going on at the feet of Tezcatlipoca and another to convey her information to Zilpan. Now she ascended to the upper room once more, and with bated breath watched the ceremonial there until the scarlet capes were let down. It was the signal for which she had been waiting. She flew down to the black apartment and from that moment on had no other thought than for Zilpan.

"Strike!" she cried to him across all that intervening space that still yawned between her and her love. "Strike! The scarlet capes of the priests have fallen. Izon is battling for his life!" Bursting from the palanquin, Zilpan rushed through the column, knocking down several soldiers who inadvertently stood in his way, until seeing Don Raymon who was standing on an elevated jutting crag in the front, directing the development of his forces, he shouted, "Señor! Izon is fighting on the teocolli!"

BATTLE AT THE GATES

"Strike, soldiers of Luxtol!" commanded Don Raymon. "Strike for God and Izon!"

And they did strike. Through the gates of the Pearl City wall there came with loud battle yells the van of Luxtol, dragging with clanking, ponderous roll, its middle supported upon wheels, a huge beam with a head of black stone as hard as steel. A withering storm of arrows and stones from catapults showered upon the soldiers as the head of the battering ram was hurled against the Red City gates, and a score of them dropped in their tracks. Nothing daunted, the backward rush began. Fresh men sprang up to take the places of those that had fallen, and again the huge battering ram crashed against the gates. Again and again the ponderous beam swept forward, every handle grasped by eager volunteers, and with every stroke the gates groaned and splintered and weakened more and more, until Gautemotzin, perched upon the walls above the gate, shrieked furious imprecations upon the attacking party, realizing the resistless force of this new and mighty machine which had been evolved in the Pearl City. From behind the battering ram a shower of arrows and missiles from spring guns struck the defenders upon the wall, mowing them down, and Gautemotzin, as yet unscathed but unable to stand it longer, leaped from the bold position where he had defied the marksmen of the attacking party and suddenly threw open the great gates, just as the ram came rushing on for the stroke that would have splintered them. Surprised by the absence of the impact for which they had braced, the crew of the battering engine were forced onward by its momentum, carrying the ram far through the gates, and then, while his men cut down the invaders with yells of triumph, the giant leader attempted to shut the gates with the engine inside. It was a clever ruse, but it failed, for the gates, battered until their fastenings dragged, would not shut again, and the forces of Luxtol rushed in under an avalanche of arrows and rocks.

It was a hand-to-hand conflict now, for the most part, although Don Raymon saw with chagrin the thousands of arrows wasted on the cliffs by his archers because they were in the rear. Suddenly recalling the tactics of Duke William at the battle of Hastings, he summoned the chiefs of the archers and ordered them to have their men shoot their arrows upward, and in a few minutes

BATTLE AT THE GATES

a shower of death fell upon his foes. In the front the shelf of the cliff was narrow and the fighting was so fierce that many warriors, because of the contracted footing of the battleground, were crowded too near the brink, and many even without scar or bruise of battle, were forced over the edge of the chasm to find death in the river, which never, since the first invasion of the Aztecs upon its domain, had been so surfeited with human lives.

Where the two forces clashed, men reached the coveted front of the fighting but to die, and, where that gory line wavered, the narrow space lay piled with dead and dying so high that they formed one barricade after another; but always it was the intrepid warriors led by Don Raymon who captured these barricades and formed new ones. On both sides there arose individual heroes, men to whom death seemed to have granted a special immunity, and these, ever in the thickest of the fighting, stained crimson from head to foot, hoarse and almost voiceless from the continued cries of encouragement and defiance that they shouted, arose like invincible demons of warfare above the human ramparts that were forming like winrows of grain. Hundreds of such fighters unable to get to the front through the struggling mass ahead of them, climbed, some up and others down the cliffs where, clinging with one hand, they met their foes in similar positions. Thus the canyon walls from the banks of the river to the upper plateau was the scene of deadly hand-to-hand duels, each of which ended with such savage shouts of triumph, that a pandemonium-like roar echoed from the opposite walls!

Among those most daring, most insensible to self, most set on endless vengeance upon all the hordes of the Red City, was a slight pale youth without armor, into whose weak frame there had suddenly come the mighty strength of battle frenzy,—Ziplan. Securing a spear from a fallen soldier, with the long-pent-up passion of his wrongs surging in his veins, he forced his way to the front as if, single-handed, he would cut his way through all opposition, defying man and fate and even death, until he found that other self — that self which he had been taught from infancy to be a love that was a part of every life; and with every stroke he cried the name of Azra.

Tezcotzin, as the chief of the leading Luxtol battalion, now seized his opportunity for revenge upon

BATTLE AT THE GATES

Gautemotzin. He had struggled madly to reach his treacherous foe of the gantlet. Urging Don Raymon to cease exposing himself so recklessly, Tezcotzin now led the onslaught; it was he who fought in the van of every fresh advance; it was he who finally forced the last great charge which beat back the army of raving pagans until his men gained the deserted battering ram, which, since its capture, had stood merely as an impediment in the centre of the road. But now that it was gained, the ram became once more an engine of destruction.

By pulling a rod that ran through its centre there flashed forth on each side sharp blades that had been sheathed within, and now, as it was again rolled forward, it mowed down the forces of Ixtol like a scythe. Against this terrible weapon the Red City soldiers fell back aghast, and their stubborn defence became a rout.

Gautemotzin alone refused to give way before its resistless onslaught. As it neared him he sprang upon it and, brandishing his sword, ran back upon the huge beam where Tezcotzin was bent now to this new devastation. Nerved by a madness born of the fierce torture to which he had been subjected, Tezcotzin for the moment saw only his great enemy. As he was at the very end of the ram and had its guidance, he suddenly swerved and ran the strange car of death straight for the cliff, a curve of which they were now rounding. It was all done in an instant, and the momentum of the ponderous machine was too great to overcome, so the men who were propelling it released their hold to save their lives and let it go down to destruction. Gautemotzin, just beyond its middle, his eyes blazing his hatred, stood above the chasm, a stalwart figure, holding his reddened sword aloft in the sunshine. For that instant the long beam of the battering ram seemed motionless, and then it suddenly pitched forward. Gautemotzin leaped for the cliff. The momentum of the ram was against him, and he landed on the very edge of the precipice. He stood, poised for a moment as he cast his sword in a flashing whirl behind him in his effort to gain a balance. It was vain, and as he began to fall backward, he turned and with a defiant yell, sprang out into the air, thence down into the gorge which swallowed him as if he had never been.

Panic-stricken, the soldiers of the Red City were still retreating, and the victorious warriors of Luxtol pressed closely upon them, harassing their flight, pick-

BATTLE AT THE GATES

ing off the laggards with ruthless hand, plunging after them, undaunted, into the blackness that had settled down, like a pall, over the city of vices. Up to the very base of the teocolli the chase continued, through darkness and lightning and crashing thunder. As they neared it, Father Zolcoma, who though a non-combatant had been swept along by the mighty human torrent, took the lead at the side of Don Raymon, calling loudly upon the name of Izon, having it in his mind to scale the teocolli itself and, if it were not too late, to wrest Izon from the grasp of the priests. As for Zilpan, as his footsteps came upon the plaza, the fever of the battle left him and a new impulse swept in upon him, took possession of him body and spirit, captured all his sense and all his soul. Azra! She was near him! He could feel her very presence, pressing closer, through the darkness and the turmoil, as surely as the unseeing needle turns unerringly to the pole.

Aye, and she was near him. Flying down from her tower, whence all the guards that had hemmed her in had fled, unable longer to wait for his coming as he approached through that drenching baptism of blood, she threaded her way without hesitation through all the confused and shrieking mob and through the sky blackness, straight to her goal. She was not seeking Zilpan, she was merely going to him. The same marvellous sense which had been born in them through Topeltzin's careful study and teaching, now guided them as surely as the sun and moon are guided in their courses in the heavens, and there, in the midst of that pandemonium, surrounded by that maelstrom of the worst passions of which humanity is capable, these two who had loved with a more exquisite and more intense love than would be good for the mass of frail humanity, threw themselves into each other's arms and sank down in sighing faintness at the first buttress of the bridge, where good fortune sheltered them from the flying feet of the rabble.

But now disaster came upon the army of the Pearl City in a strange and unexpected manner. The plaza was crowded with a frightened throng, and as the soldiers of Topeltzin poured into it with the intention of forming into defensive array at the base of the teocolli, they became inextricably confused with that fear-crazed mass of spectators. Therefore, as Don Raymon's forces came up they found themselves confronted with a de-

BATTLE AT THE GATES

fence so unexpected and at the same time so effective that all their plans and all their prowess went for naught. This unwitting defence was nothing more than the passive mob itself, soft, unresisting, mere sheep — helpless masses of flesh into which swords might plunge and plunge again and carve no onward pathway.

Feeling that pursuit had been checked and discovering the reason, the soldiers of the Red City took fresh heart and began to press forward, pushing the rabble before them, a sickening human bulwark that was impervious to assault and scaling. The constantly flashing lightning now showed pale, terrified, piteous faces, upturned as if in supplication to the inky sky, and to mow these faces down was a butchery that took the heart out of the bravest and most ruthless alike. The lines of Don Raymon wavered and gave way, beaten back step by step by the mere mass of non-combatants that, bound in upon the roadway by the cliff on one side and the chasm on the other, could be slain but not destroyed because of their very numbers. In spite of rally after rally, the soldiers of Luxtol, unwilling to slay unarmed people, were forced by one of the strangest circumstances that ever occurred in warfare, to retreat constantly, past curve after curve in the narrow street, to just beyond the outskirts of the city proper.

And here all strife ceased by still another strange happening. There came a sudden slight tremor of the earth, and then, without warning, almost, with merely a sharp, crackling report, a portion of the cliff-shelf upon which the roadway wound, slid down into the abyss, carrying with it many of the soldiers and citizens of the Red City, and leaving the army of rescue cut off from the army of defence by a dark, impassable chasm that with startling swiftness had opened before their very feet. And across that chasm Father Zolcoma and Don Raymon were left amid their followers, straining their eyes into the blackness and calling aloud to heaven for aid for the now hopeless and helpless quartet upon the top of the teocolli.

CHAPTER XL

ON THE TEOCOLLI — OMNIPOTENCE

WITH a scream of despair Isabel seized the long hair of the priest who held her and twisted it around her arms and hands, determined to defend herself to the utmost. Mariam lay in a faint on the parapet, while her assailant was struggling with Zeno. The parapet was some three feet thick, which made it no easy task to cast over a vigorous, struggling young woman, and as Isabel's captor was frantically trying to break her hold, she dimly saw the ravening horde close in on Black Eagle and Izon. Black Eagle, his spear and knife both gone, stood in front of Izon, receiving with indifference the blows which were being showered upon his mail-clad body. He had thrown up his visor and Isabel saw his despairing look directed toward her; she saw, too, in Izon's face, his awful agony.

With a howl of mingled pain and triumph Isabel's captor tore his hair from her grasp. Zeno was struck down and both girls lifted to the parapet. At this sight a berserker frenzy possessed Black Eagle. With mad roars he flung himself down from the stone, hurling his armor-weighted bulk against the priests, his mailed legs and arms, like heavy swingles, striking and gyrating with a rapidity that would have made a whirling dervish look still, but steadily moving towards the girls, a blood-mad, human cyclone! Topeltzin, with a gloating yell, ordered every priest except the captors of the girls to surround the chieftain, and it was thus for a moment that Izon was alone. His first impulse was to follow and help his friend but he paused overwhelmed by a tremendous conviction. Like Diomed of the purged vision, who could see the gods in the upper air, taking sides with the Greeks and the Trojans, he perceived in the gathering canyon storm the unsheathing sword of the Almighty. He felt that further human effort was vain. His pride in his physical prowess was crushed. He realized at last that the triumphing powers of evil could be conquered by their Master alone. Thus inspired, he suddenly hurled his sword at the priests. The heavy basket-hilt of the whirling weapon struck the head of one wretch, whose dying yell, as he fell, was drowned in the pandemonium of the fighting. Izon, uttering no sound, but with a heart swelling with reverence and awe, sank to his knees upon the gory altar of Satan, his bare and blood-splotched arms raised in humble supplication.

A blazing flash of lightning blinded them all with its lurid glare, to be instantly followed by a crash of thunder which rolled and reverberated through the canyoñ like the bellowing of a million hell-loosed demons. With magical swiftness the black cloud enveloped everything in fearful darkness, to be lit up only by the flashing of the incessant lightning. Isabel and Mariam could feel their captors trembling with terror, for the temple was shaking dangerously. All that were upon the teocolli were so startled by the sudden glare and crash that they ceased movement. As the reverberations of the thunder rolled away, there ensued a moment of tense silence in which came the distant chant—

"*Sanctus! Sanctus! Dominus Deus Sabaoth! Pleni sunt coeli!*"

Topeltzin, crouching against the parapet where he had shrunk during the lightning, sprang forward in renewed fury at the sound. "Strike! you cowards!" he howled — "leave Izon — kill the Indian — hurl the women over!"

Izon, still kneeling, and thrilled with the hosannas

PRINCE IZON

that reverberated down the canyon, was suddenly seized with a premonition that Omnipotence was about to strike! He leapt from the stone as shot from a catapult, and flung himself upon the priests who were howling around Black Eagle like hounds about a stag. Goaded by Topeltzin, they closed with frantic shrieks on the two warriors. Shouting to Black Eagle, "Down, down to the pavement," Izon grasped two of the priests, and as he threw them, he fell also. Black Eagle, knowing only that there was some good reason for the command, instantly flung himself against a group of his foes, going down with them, and in a moment both he and Izon were covered by the howling, struggling mass. Topeltzin sprang forward with upraised obsidian knife. For an instant he was unable to strike without danger to the priests. In that instant Mariam and Isabel were raised for the final plunge. Breathing a last prayer, as they faced the sky, it was vouchsafed to the awed sight of these tortured girls to behold a transcendent vision. Like a colossal curtain parted by invisible might, the cloud rolled back, and the heavens extending into infinity, were illumined with an ineffable radiance. From the apex of the empyrean, hurled upon its errand of

ON THE TEOCOLLI

death, came a dazzling bolt, striking the idol with a deafening crash, and shattering it to pieces upon the struggling priests that covered the prince and the chieftain!

The stillness of death ensued as black darkness instantly enveloped them. No sound came from even the wounded priests writhing in agony. A new horror paralyzed all, as the swaying and heaving of the teocolli in an earthquake presaged its fall. The captors of the fainting girls sank under them in terror, while Topeltzin was thrown stunned against the parapet.

It was Izon who first grasped the significance of the catastrophe — at which he was not surprised — and calling to Black Eagle the two, both wounded, freed themselves from the mass of stricken and stunned priests covering them, and even from limbs that clung to them in the grip of death.

"Come!" cried Izon. "Down to the plaza!"

He and Black Eagle grasped Mariam and Isabel, guided by the recurrent lightning. Topeltzin was upon the other side of the stone, and though weakened by his wound, dashed forward to intercept them, but he tripped and fell face forward upon the ruins that had buried his priests. Down the winding pathway sped the escaping quartet, but they had not made more than two convolutions when they heard a scream of bitter rage from the temple top. Topeltzin and the last two priests were rushing after them, bent upon their murder. It was a terrible race around and down the sides of the rocking teocolli. The lightning flashed continuously, and reverberations of the thunder were increasing. Topeltzin, however, wounded as he was, was not able to make the speed that he might otherwise have put forth, or the two men, encumbered by the girls and almost exhausted by their exertions and injuries, would surely have been overtaken one by one, and as they were unarmed and the three priests carried their knives, they might have fallen victims after all. As it was, however, they gained the base of the teocolli in safety. They found that portion of the plaza empty. The Red City soldiers by pressing the mob ahead of them, had forced Don Raymon's men back. The four were almost in as desperate a position as before, for not one friend was within call, and Topeltzin was but a few paces behind them.

ON THE TEOCOLLI

The high priest dashed after them across the plaza in mad fury. But he suddenly paused. A mighty upheaval had taken place in that instant, and not one living soul within all the canyon moved! This terror came from beneath and it was one that they could not escape. With a tremendous roar the teocolli suddenly toppled over, its thousands of tons of rock plunging down with a mighty crash, carrying the last two priests into the depths of the canyon. Chaos had come! On every hand buildings were toppling from their foundations, were falling forward and bounding, huge masses of shapeless, broken rock, from terrace to cliff, and from cliff to terrace. Great fissures gaped beneath the feet and one of them left Topeltzin separated from all humanity by a yawning width from which came sulphurous fumes. An earthquake had seized and devastated the Red City. Flying rocks and *débris* filled the air, and citizens and nobles, priests and soldiers, maids and matrons, tottering graybeards and children were buried under the avalanche. After that first dreadful shock which paralyzed every faculty, men and women were seen dashing for their very lives in every direction. Deep black crevices opened in the cliffs where palaces

PRINCE IZON

that had once stood in all the bravery of their carven stone and golden overlay, were now heaps of tumbled and scattered ruins, heaved constantly apart by new vibrations, to bound forward and downward until they finally found their resting place in the choking and foaming river.

In some places whole sections of the cliff had fallen forward. An entire battalion of Topeltzin's soldiers lay buried under his own palace, and others, his entire army, the army which he had built up with such pride, picked from the highest and the lowest of his dominions for their splendid physique, lay scattered, and crushed beneath masses of granite, along the main highway, whence they had pursued Don Raymon's soldiers. Among them, as repulsive as the coarsest soldiers in their mangled denial of any resemblance to human kind, lay the fair flower girls, the graceful dancers, the lissome Tequiepa, all the enticing beauties of the voluptuous court, and in those depths also rested Zilpan and Azra; but these last were more blessed than all the rest so far as the affairs of this earth are concerned, for they had stepped into eternity in the very midst of the highest

ON THE TEOCOLLI

bliss that had come into their poor lives, the ecstasy of love in reunion.

The ruin was complete! The time of reckoning had come to the city of consummate wickedness. Omnipotence had spoken and spoken in no uncertain tones, and the four fugitives knelt in the plaza offering their profoundest gratitude.

They knelt just out of reach of Topeltzin who, unawed even by this evidence of supreme power, stood cursing his defiance at the tremendous forces of nature itself, in his impotent wrath an epitome of all man's puny weakness, his boasted strength but as the flutterings of a feeble insect in the face of this mighty destruction. Still his impious soul would not bend, and still he raved out imprecations against all the powers that dwelt in earth or air or in the heavens above, shaking his fists at the inky sky out of which still came those flashes of lightning which now served but to illuminate the appalling scene.

And it was a scene terrible to behold. But a short hour before the glorious Red City had lain smiling under the bright sunlight, its ornate structures proudly reared

PRINCE IZON

toward the heavens and facing the fairest stretch of gardens and groves that had ever been constructed by man. Along two solid miles the proud city had spread its triumphs of architectural wealth, and now, in the frightful gleams of the lightning, where these magnificent buildings had stood were only scarred places in the cliffs, chaotic masses that had been riven and scattered into their primeval rubbish. The hand of the Almighty had pressed down in just wrath long restrained and had brushed the work of centuries down into the canyon like worthless dust, in as complete and terrible a destruction as that which descended upon Pompeii and Herculaneum.

It was hard to stand in the midst of this cataclysm and to think that, overhead and beyond those pitch-black clouds, still shone a benign sun, but it was so. That same sun beamed down in all its splendor upon the pure, clean façades of the beautiful Pearl City whose dwellers now looked from afar in wonder at the terrible storm which raged in the canyon below them. It was difficult for those of Prince Izon's little band to gaze upon this desolate sight through the angry lightnings and believe that all its former splendor was gone; and

ON THE TEOCOLLI

it was impossible for them to see into the future to that happy day when Mariam and Prince Izon would reign in the love of their subjects of Pearl City, with Don Raymon and Father Zolcoma as their chief counsellors, and when Black Eagle and Isabel should have realized that fulness of joy that comes from perfect union.

CHAPTER XLI

THE LAST VICTIM

THE Cross! By some means, the wind that now swept down the canyon opened a way through the black clouds which, though they still hung thickly over the doomed city, now parted enough to reveal a portion of the upper canyon, and there, high in the air, where the sun shone bright and sparkling upon it, loomed that golden beacon of hope. Nothing else could be seen. It seemed to be hung there, suspended radiantly in the air, n emblem of that omnipotence which shall exist forever and forever. It seemed, in that bright burnishing, to lose the effect of distance, to be brought quite close to them, hovering over the five as a benediction, and over the one solitary figure, that stood raving at the base of the fallen teocolli, as a menace. Topeltzin gazed up at it now for the first time in his life in awe. It seemed to him the symbol of all the destruction of his works, the uprooting of all his impious plans, the barrier between him and his demoniacal de-

THE LAST VICTIM

sires, the downfall of his god; and in that moment of awe doom came upon him.

The palace of Topeltzin had been rent and riven from end to end and from front to back; not one apartment that was built above the cliff or tunnelled into its sides had been left intact. Even dungeon cells were rent asunder, and poor maimed creatures, under his stern lock and key, were set loose, only to have the roofs and walls of their confines bury them again. Only one prisoner whose cell was jarred open was spared, and he was a moaning wretch who had lost tongue and nose and ears, and out of whose piteous scarred face there gleamed but one indomitable eye.

He found himself perched upon the cliff-side alone, and mechanically scrambled forward among the crumbled rubbish until he found himself at the side of the only work of man that still held its head erect. He had come forth upon the level of the banquet hall, where the huge, towering golden statue of Tezcatlipoca gazed out upon the scenes of desolation below. Topeltzin stood almost directly beneath this spot, and the brawny figure that was once Captain Helox, gazing down astounded at the devastation, distinguished his heartless tormentor in the glare of the lightning. Almost he had an impulse to throw himself forward from that dizzy height upon the detested figure, but a swaying of the ponderous statue gave him another thought. Examining it he saw that it was tilted forward at a perilous angle, that it was almost pivoted upon the front edge of its base, that behind it rocks and walls from above had formed into a solid mass. The stumps of his arms hindered him, but with painful manœuvrings he managed to scramble up in the rear of the statue, and, with his back pressed firmly against it, placed his feet against the solid mass behind it. He pushed with all his might, the great muscles of his back straining until he feared they would crush his bones by their mighty tension. His great limbs quivered with the force that he put into them; the veins in his temples throbbed painfully and still he exerted more strength. He could feel all the force of his will and all the strength of his spirit oozing from him into muscular action, and he was almost swooning with the surrender of strength to the one supreme effort. The statue swayed, it inclined forward in answer to that mighty thrust, until finally it toppled and fell crashing forward; and in that moment in which

THE LAST VICTIM

he felt it giving way the great heart of Captain Helox broke and he dropped down upon the now deserted base of the statue.

The watchers below, Izon and Mariam, Black Eagle and Isabel, caught the first cracking sound of that tearing away and looked up aghast. They cried out, but Topeltzin, his eyes still fixed upon that gleaming cross, did not hear them and would not have understood them if he had. Even as they shrieked, the statue came hurtling down through the air, the gleaming of lightning upon it giving it all the effect of a gigantic fiery bolt hurled out of an inky sky. Down, down, down, it came with awful precision to where Topeltzin stood with his eyes still upturned to that mighty symbol that had overthrown him. With a hollow roar it fell squarely upon him, flattening him to the earth with all his burden of sins upon his soul; and, the head of the statue falling over the edge of the dark chasm, it lay there, its garnet eyes gazing deep down into that fell abyss as if aghast at all the stricken splendors of the Red City that had gone to destruction within its depths!

THE END

www.ingramcontent.com/pod-product-compliance
Lightning Source LLC
Chambersburg PA
CBHW030344190426
43201CB00041B/88